On Angels' Wings: Or The Story Of A Little Violet Of Edelsheim

Louisa Lilias Greene

ON ANGELS' WINGS;

OR,

The Story of Little Violet of Edelsheim.

By the

HON^BLE. MRS. GREENE,

Author of " The Grey House on the Hill," " The Babe i' the Mill,"
&c. &c.

WITH ILLUSTRATIONS

London:
T. NELSON AND SONS, PATERNOSTER ROW.
EDINBURGH; AND NEW YORK.

1885.

ON ANGELS' WINGS.

A PERILOUS POSITION.

Page 276.

THOMAS NELSON AND SONS,
London, Edinburgh, and New York.

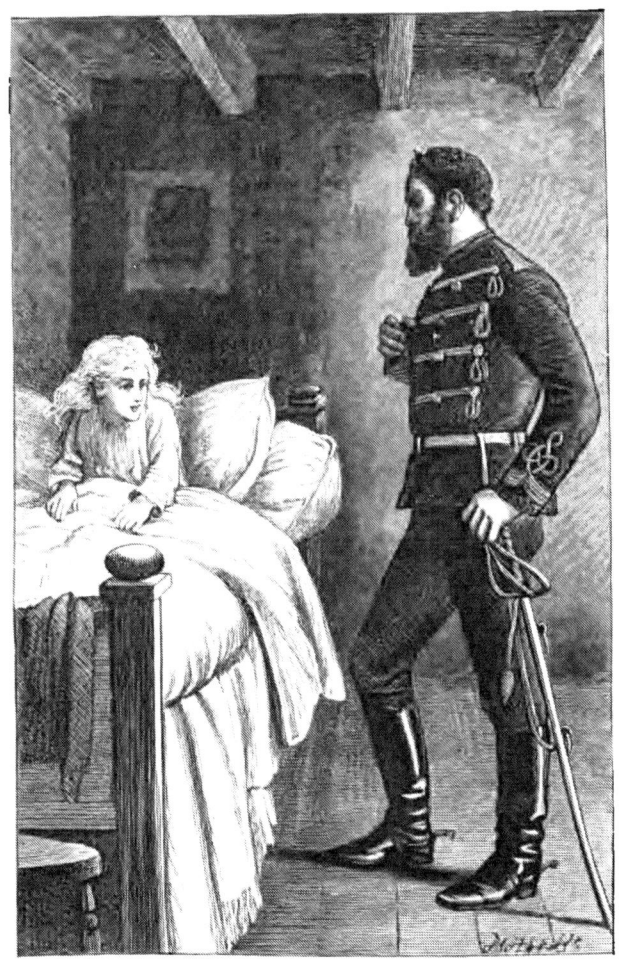

VIOLET'S SURPRISE.

Page 89.

Contents.

ON ANGELS' WINGS.

CHAPTER I.

LITTLE VIOLET.

EVERY one knew little Violet. She sat always in a small window which projected out over the street, and her purple frock and pale face were looked for and recognized by almost every passer-by.

She had sat in that curious turret-shaped window for four years—in winter, in spring, in summer, in autumn. Other children made snow men and pelted snowballs in the street beneath, while she looked on from above and laughed and clapped her hands. In the spring the little ones went off by the score and gathered yellow and purple crocuses, of which not a few found their way into Violet's lap, or bloomed again in the vases which stood on the sills of the old-fashioned eight-sided window. She loved to have those flowers,

and took them from the children's hands with her
brightest and most grateful smile.   Later on they
brought her violets, sweet wood-violets, and trailing
ground-ivy; but for these flowers she now had no
smile, only tears, which gathered and multiplied, and
which would, despite all her efforts, run down her
purple dress in large, bright drops.   For was not she
herself called Violet? and had not some one, not so
long ago, often whispered this word to her in a voice
which seemed for ever in her ears?—

" My own sweet Violet, lay thy head on mother's
breast and rest thee a while.   My little Violet is
sweeter to me than all the flowers in the town."

And now that Violet had no mother, she could
scarcely bear to look at the purple blossoms which
they brought to her in bunches; and yet she put them
aside, and, when they were withered, treasured them all
in " mother's Bible," which lay always on a little table
beside her.

In summer, in the gap at the far end of the street,
between the church and the fountain, she could always
catch a glimpse of the hills—the beautiful green hills,
covered with trees to the very top, and from whence,
in the autumn, the children returned laden with nuts,
baskets and satchels and boxes full; and though
Violet did not eat nuts, they made tea-things out of

the shells, and had doll tea-parties in the old turret-window.

A year ago she had been a very happy little girl; and although even then she could not walk, nor run, nor jump about like other children, still she never fretted about it. She had some one always with her who made the long days pass so happily, that she never stopped to ask herself why she was unlike the others, or why all the neighbours as they went by looked up at her with such pity in their eyes.

Only once for a few moments she had seemed to understand something about it, when little Fritz Adler, her great friend, going by riding on a stick with a horse's head attached to it, shrieked up to her from the street beneath in great pride,—

"Ha, ha, Violet! look at me how I can prance; thou couldst not do so if thou triedst."

"I could," she shouted. "By-and-by, when I can run like thee, I will ride too."

"No, no, thou never wilt," screamed Fritz, giving his wooden horse a lash with his leather whip. "I wanted to give thee this horse, this very one; Ella had bought thee this very whip; but mother said 'No,' it would be folly to give thee such a present."

"Why?" asked Violet. "Why, Fritz, did she say that?"

"Ah! thou knowest thou art not like other children."

"Why am not I like other children?"

"Because thou canst not run or even walk about like me and Ella. Mother says thou art a little hunchback, and it would hurt thy poor back to ride and prance like this;" and Fritz, again lashing his horse, began to plunge violently up and down on the pavement opposite.

"Fritz, what didst thou say? I am what?" but he could give no answer, for his mother, who lived in the little baker's shop across the road, rushing out, promptly secured the offender, and having given him a smart slap across the face, dragged him back into the house.

"Mother, what did he say I was? and why did his mother slap him? He called me a little hunch-back. What does that mean, mother?"

Violet's mother had not been attending to the conversation. She had been working at a little white frilled pinafore for her daughter at a table near the stove, and she had just taken the crimping irons from the heart of the fire, red-hot and smoking; but when she heard these words she dropped them suddenly on the floor, and in a moment she was on her knees in front of little Violet's chair, and covering the child's thin white hands with kisses.

" What does it signify what it means; he is a cruel boy to call thee such a name. Thou art my darling, my treasure, my sweetest Violet. Thou art the most precious little girl in all the town."

Somewhat amazed at her mother's sudden anguish of mind, and at the passionate way she kissed her cheeks and stroked her hair, Violet gazed at her with eyes which widened and dilated, and then she seemed for a few moments lost in thought; after which she said, in her usual quiet voice, with only the faintest tinge of trouble in it,—

" Mother, dear, is this a hump I have on my back ? and is that the reason why I sit in this chair and cannot walk ?"

" Dearest," replied her mother almost in a whisper, " my heart's love, do not fret or think any more about what Fritz said. Thou art one of God's own little children, and is not that the best thing of all ?"

Violet nodded her head—it was a way she had of agreeing to things said to her; but still she was not quite satisfied, for after a pause she said anxiously,—

" But did God give me this hump, mother ? and what is in it that it pains me so ?"

As she asked this question, she gave a sudden sob,

and some tears fell on the front of her pretty purple dress.

"Do not cry, my sweetest treasure," cried the mother, drawing the child's head down on her shoulder, and once more covering it with kisses. "What does it matter what we are like here? If thou canst not walk nor run here, by-and-by Christ will carry my little lamb in his bosom; and if thou hast a hump on thy back now, what does it matter? Some day the good Lord Jesus will call my little one to himself, and then all the pain will be gone; and where the poor shoulders ache so much now, thou wilt have wings, shining wings, and thou wilt never cry there any more, but always be quite happy."

"And Violet will have wings!—thou knowest that?" said the little girl, lifting her head suddenly from her mother's shoulder and looking earnestly into her face.

"Yes, darling."

"Beautiful, shining, silver wings; and no more hump and no more pain?"

"No more hump and no more pain," replied her mother softly.

"And thou wilt be there, dearest mother?"

"Yes, sweetest treasure, I trust I shall be there."

"And father?"

" And father also."

" And Fritz; will he be there ? Will he not, mother ?"

" I hope so. Yes; but it was not kind of him to speak roughly to my little one."

" His mother slapped him," said Violet sorrowfully.

" He deserved it," replied her mother somewhat sharply.

The little girl gave a long sigh; and pressing one of the tears which still stood in a bright drop on the front of her dress with the tip of her finger until it disappeared in the purple cashmere folds, she said softly,—

" I love Fritz. I must tell him what thou hast just told me, that though I cannot run or jump like him or Ella, some day, not very far away, when the Lord Jesus calls me, I shall have wings. Is it not true, mother ?"

" Quite true," she answered with an effort, then turned quickly away towards the stove and resumed her ironing.

CHAPTER II.

A YEAR had flown away since that eventful day when Fritz had somewhat roughly awakened Violet to the fact that she was a little hunchback, and that she was never to run or walk like him or Ella; and now everything connected with this little life of hers was changed. The young mother with the fair hair and the blue eyes and the warm, loving heart, had flown away before her little girl. The good Lord Jesus had called her first, and she was asleep now in the little churchyard beside the church which stood at the end of the street.

She could not shelter nor protect her little girl any more from hurtful words, nor press her to her heart to soothe the pain which they had caused her. She could not sit beside her in the window and read and talk to her till the hours flew by almost unnoticed, so that Violet often forgot that her back ached and that her legs were weary.

(789)

It had come so suddenly too—at least to Violet it was sudden. She had not noticed the short coughs, or the quick breathing, or the flushed cheeks; only to her eyes her little mother, as she always called her, grew more lovely every day. But one night when she was asleep, and dreaming of a wooden go-cart which Fritz had promised to make for her the next day, her father came to her bedside and called to her to awake.

"Violet, my darling, thou must awake. Come with me to thy mother; she is calling for thee."

"For me," she said, rising up with sleepy eyes and tossed hair. "Where is dear mother, and why does she want me in the night?"

Her father stooped down over the bed and lifted her up in his arms very gently, for it hurt her to lift her up quickly or roughly; and without answering her he carried her through the doorway into the inner room.

"Mother, dear, why dost thou want me in the night?" asked Violet, sleepily stretching out her arms towards the bed in which her mother lay.

"Is it night?" she replied in a voice which sounded quite strange to the little girl's ears. "John, where is my darling? I cannot see her; put her here, close beside me.—There, sweetest one; lay thy head on mother's breast."

Violet placed her head on her mother's shoulder, and stretching out her little arm, threw it lovingly round her neck. "What ails sweet mother?" she said softly. "Art thou sick?"

"Ay, sick unto death. Mother has sent for her little girl to bid her good-bye. Mother must say adieu to her poor sick girlie; but father will love thee, oh, so well.—Is it not so, beloved? Thou hast always been better to her than many mothers."

"Yes, yes," he said huskily; "never fear, thou knowest that I love her."

"And by-and-by she will follow me to heaven. Is it not so, John? She will be glad to find me there."

"Yes, darling, yes. And now kiss thy little one, and I will carry her back to bed;" for the childish eyes were beginning to dilate with a strange terror, and Violet was shrinking nervously back against the wall.

"Good-bye, good-bye, good-bye," cried the poor mother, clinging to the little white figure as John lifted her from the bed; "when Violet has wings she will fly to her dear mother in heaven, will she not?"

"Yes," replied Violet, her face brightening up with a broad, sweet smile as her father lifted her in his

arms, and she leaned her cheek against his, " beautiful silver wings ; but mother must not go to heaven
to-night, for to-morrow Fritz is to bring me my cart,
and mother has promised to put a cushion in it and
wheel Violet round the room."

Her father carried her back to her bed and laid
her down, oh, so softly and tenderly, and kissed her
with a long kiss, longer than any he had ever given
her before, and then he went back into the room and
closed the door.   Violet did not hear anything more.
She looked for some time at the beautiful purple sky
outside, filled with thousands of shining stars.   She
saw the roofs of the houses with their pointed gables ;
and on the top of the chimney opposite she could see
the grave figure of a stork standing upright in the
starlight beside its nest.   She felt sad at first and
trembled a little, she did not know why.   For why
had her mother called her in the middle of the
night and said good-bye to her ?   Where was she
going ?   She had never gone away anywhere from
her before, and to-morrow she had promised to give
her that ride in Fritz's cart, and to tell her again that
story about the cruel tailor who ran his needle into
the elephant's trunk ; and Violet smiled and forgot her
troubles as she remembered how the elephant filled
his great trunk at the gutter and splashed it all over

the tailor as he sat cross-legged at his work in the open window; and soon, her mind growing more composed, and somewhat tangled with sleep, she thought she heard the tailor crying somewhere outside in the street. She did not like to hear him sobbing; and every time she looked up, the elephant was still shooting up water into the air; but the bright drops which she saw were the stars still twinkling on the dark back-ground of the sky, and the sobbing came from the next room, where her father was kneeling brokenhearted by the bedside on which her little mother lay dead.

CHAPTER III.

A SAD DISCOVERY.

It was not for many days that Violet understood that
her mother was really dead; perhaps, indeed, she did
not quite understand it for many months to come.
It seemed so strange to her that in the morning when
she opened her eyes her father was boiling the kettle
on the stove, and arranging the little wooden tray,
which was always laid on her bed, with her morning
meal, hot and tempting, placed upon it. It was he,
too, who, lifting her gently up, placed the pillows
behind her poor tired shoulders, and propped up her
back so that she could sit forward and eat her egg
and the sweet rolls which the baker sent across the
street every day, fresh and smoking, for her breakfast.

" Where is mother ? " she asked each morning with
a little sorrowful smile; for her father was so good
and kind, and he sat so patiently beside her bed, and
buttered the bread with such care that she did not

want to cry or sob, though there was such a lump in her throat that she could not swallow what he gave her. " Where is mother, dear father ? She did not come to see me all yesterday."

" She was not able to come," he said in a low voice.

" But where is she ? Is she in the next room ? "

John bowed his head over the tray, but made no answer. " Here, eat thy egg, little one; it will be cold."

" Mother always lifts the top off for me," said she with a sob.

" Ah, so she does. I am afraid father is a poor old stupid, is he not ? "

She looked up hurriedly, her father's voice sounded so strangely and his fingers trembled as he tried clumsily to lift the white top off the egg. Then she saw that tears were streaming down her father's face and trickling down his beard; and thinking she had pained him by her words, she threw her arms around his neck and cried out sorrowfully,—

" Thou best father, thou art not a bit stupid. I love thee, oh so much. The breakfast is too nice; only mother always eats a piece of my cake and drinks some of the milk, and thou must do so too."

" Yes, yes, of course." John drew his hand hastily

across his face, and broke off a piece of the cake. He drank a mouthful of the milk, and then quickly rising, he laid the piece of cake on the table by the stove, and went into the other room.

It was the next day that Violet was told the truth, though the truth was to remain to her for many a long day a strange and cruel mystery. When she opened her eyes at the usual hour the following morning her father was not there, and only old Kate the servant, who waited on all the various lodgers in John's house, was in the room, standing by the stove, and pouring some water into a saucepan.

" Where is father ? " asked Violet, raising herself up painfully in the bed, and gazing around her with a frightened air.

" He has gone out," replied Kate, keeping her back turned towards the child. " Go to sleep. He said I was not to wake thee till he came home."

" But I am awake."

" Never mind ; thou must go to sleep again. He said thou wert on no account to awake or to speak until he returned."

" But I cannot go to sleep again," cried Violet, beginning to whimper a little. " I can never go to sleep again in the mornings unless mother lifts me up in the bed and settles my pillows. Is mother gone out too? She has not come in these three mornings to see me."

Kate did not answer the question, for at this moment she had upset some of the water out of the saucepan upon the top of the stove, and it frizzled and made a great hissing and noise.

Meanwhile Violet had raised herself upon her elbow, and was gazing steadily at the door of her mother's room.

"Kate," she said presently, in a low, coaxing voice, "couldst thou not carry me in thy arms in there? I know thou art very old, but father always says I am not heavier than a fly."

"Thy father would be very angry if I were to attempt to carry thee. He is far too careful of thee to trust thee to my old bones."

"But thou must do it, Kate." Then suddenly raising her voice till it sounded quite shrilly through the house, she cried out, "Mother, mother, may I not go into thy room? Dear mother, answer me. Violet's back aches, and she wants to lie in thy bed."

"Tush! tush!" said Kate, coming hurriedly to the bedside of the little girl, and putting her hand softly on her shoulder; "thou must not cry and clamour so, it is no use; thy mother is not in there. She cannot hear thee; thou wilt only disturb the neighbours."

" She is there, she is there. Open the door. She cannot hear me with all that noise down there in the street. Do open the door, that I may call to her."

" There is no use calling to her, poor little lamb," said Kate, sitting down on the bed beside her and wiping away her burning tears. " She cannot hear thee. They have taken her away this morning, and she will not come back any more.—The child must know the truth some time," muttered Kate uneasily to herself. " Her father should have told her before he went out."

" Why did they take her away ? " asked Violet, still all unconscious of the bitter truth conveyed by the words.

" Well, because it was arranged that she was to go this morning."

" But where—where ? Canst thou not answer me, Kate ? Canst thou not tell me where is my little mother gone ? "

" She is gone to heaven," replied Kate, turning away her head and lifting her apron to her eyes. " Poor child, why does she ask me such questions ? "

" To heaven ! " said Violet with a little start and then a long gasp of childish agony. " My mother, my own dear mother. She is not gone away, she is not gone to heaven without her little Violet ; it is so far, so far away."

"Hush, hush, child! It is not so very far away. Thou must not cry so. If thy father were to hear thee he would be angry with me that I have told thee."

"My father is not gone to heaven too?" she cried, starting up from her pillows with a fresh burst of agony. "O Kate, Kate! father will not leave his little Violet.—Father, father, come, come to Violet."

At this moment the door opened, and her father came in. His face was deadly pale, and he walked over to the bed with a look of absolute horror in his face.

"My darling, my sweet one," he cried; "here is thy father. Why dost thou call for him so? What troubles thee? What makes thee cry? Father is here now; he cannot bear to see thee weep. What ails thee, my sweetest treasure?"

"They have taken mother away out of the next room. I screamed to her, and she would not answer. And—and Kate says she will never come back to me any more."

John looked up at the old servant with questioning eyes, full of deepest anger drowned in pain.

"I could not help it, sir. The child awoke and made such a clamour I had to tell her. What wouldst thou have had me to do?" and the old woman burst into a fit of such unfeigned weeping that John uttered not a word of reproach, but turned again to soothe his little trembling darling.

"Did the good Lord Jesus call my little mother away?" asked Violet with quivering lips.

"Yes, my heart's treasure, he did," replied he hoarsely.

"And he gave her wings?"

"Yes, yes."

"And Violet is only a poor little hunchback, and has no wings; and mother said he would call me first."

John laid his head down on the pillow and sobbed.

CHAPTER IV.

FATHER'S LOVE.

IT was thus that Violet came to know that her
mother was dead; but weary days and leaden months
went by before she ceased to watch and wait for her;
and each morning she only awoke to a fresh surprise,
a fresh thrill of pain, a fresh wrestling of spirit against
what could never be altered.

While her father was in the room she seemed
always able to repress the anguish of her little heart.
He was so tender, so pitiful; he tried so earnestly to
imitate the loving ways and words of the poor dead
mother. But when he went out in the morning to
the office for his orders, or to the forest to select
wood for his trade, and his daughter was left temporarily under the charge of Kate, then it was that
all the world seemed going wrong, and that Violet's
tears flowed almost ceaselessly.

Kate had a kind, loving heart, but she had, oh,
such hard and sharp bones; and she had not learned

by long and watchful practice the easiest way to lift the poor invalid. Each day when she raised Violet from her bed and placed her in her bath before the stove, there were bitter cries of pain and sobbing cries for "mother." Kate, too, was somewhat stupid and clumsy in the matter of dressing her charge. She had long sharp nails, which often scraped her little neck and arms; and the strings of the petticoats so often got into knots, which it took tedious minutes to undo again.

Each day when John came home for his dinner at twelve, he found little Violet's eyes red with tears, and her usually pale face swelled and blotched with the traces of past grief.

"Couldst not thou dress me, father?" she had said once pitifully.

And he had promised to try; but he had not proved much more successful than Kate. The buttons of his coat had hurt her, and the strings of the little petticoats were to him an impossibility. He was a great big man, with hands like a giant; and he had a willing loving heart, bigger than his whole body, and yet the knots perplexed him even more than they did Kate; and after one trial even Violet said with a smile,—

"I am afraid father is not a very good dresser, is he?"

To which he replied with a laugh,—

"No; I am afraid father is a regular old botch."
But she saw as he turned away that there were tears
in his eyes.

After this she made no further lamentations over
her dressing. It was not that Kate improved much,
but she felt that the traces of her tears and her heavy
eyes pained her father to his very heart. She saw
it in his face each day as he entered the room at
dinner time. She saw the anxious look of inquiry,
and then the smile of relief as their eyes met, when
there were no blistered cheeks or heavy eyelids to
cause him sorrow.

Her father was by trade a wood-carver, or perhaps
more strictly speaking a toy-maker. He was wonderfully clever, and could make lovely boxes with carved
fruit and flowers on their lids; and he could design
and execute panels of cedar and walnut covered with
the most delicate traceries; but his chief employment
was making toys, jack-in-the-boxes, Noah's arks,
sheep-folds, wooden soldiers, and wooden cannon,
nine-pins, and heaps of other playthings; for the
town was famous for its toy-shops, and John worked
for one of the largest stores, and was well known to
be the most skilful hand at the trade. He had a
little workshop on the ground-floor of the house,

where he had his lathe and where he kept all his tools, and the wooden boxes also into which, when the toys were finished, he packed them for the foreign market.

In the old days, when the little mother was up-stairs, and he knew that his Violet was happy, he used to sit in this little den for hours at a time, carving and singing; while the toys which were to fill the hearts of the foreign children with delight grew under his hands in a marvellous way. But now John never sang, and the work he formerly delighted in seemed to have lost its interest. At last he thought he would bring some of his work upstairs and sit of an evening in the window of Violet's room. Of course all the lathe-work and the coarser wood-carving must be done downstairs, but he could generally find some occupation which would not litter the room above, and which did not require noisy hammering or filing.

Violet was enchanted at this new arrangement. She loved to see her father at his work, and to watch the piece of shapeless wood grow gradually under his hand into the form he wished it to assume.

Above all, she loved to see him carving the animals for the Noah's arks. When he had this work to do he always sat close up beside her in the window; and as he finished each animal he used to place it for her approval on the window-sill, until sometimes all the

narrow ledges were covered with elephants and ducks
and pigs, apparently walking along in very solemn
array.

By-and-by he allowed her to help him in his work.
He bought her a little paint-box, and he taught her
how to colour some of the animals, the yellow canaries,
the doves, and the speckled geese. He made her, too,
a little table to fit exactly in front of her chair, very
tall, with rails to it in front, on which she could
place her feet, so that when she worked she need
not lean forward to tire her back. The little birds
and foxes and squirrels which she painted were far
more beautifully coloured than those ordinarily placed
in Noah's arks, because the colours she used were
much finer than those in common use; so the good
John could say with truthful pride to the neighbours
who sometimes dropped in of an evening to chat with
him and Violet,—

"See what my little daughter can do; see how she
helps me at my work. There are no such animals to
be seen in all Edelsheim." And then Violet's pale
face would flush with pleasure, and tears, born of
happy blushes, would fill her eyes while the neighbours
looked admiringly at the yellow weasels and the little
red foxes, coloured perhaps a thought too brightly,
but still very pretty to look at.

The toys, too, with which her room was now well stocked were a great attraction to the children of the neighbourhood ; and, where guns and drums and swords were to be had for the asking, the little ones of course loved to congregate. There was beginning to be a talk now about a war with France, and the children's ideas took all of a sudden a most warlike turn. They banged the drums and blew the wooden trumpets and slashed at the chairs and tables till the din was horrible, and sometimes Violet's head ached, and she wished they would go away. But when they did go away, and the shadows grew long, and John had not returned from the forest, or was busy turning some critical work in his lathe, then she wished they were back again ; for when she was alone the old ache always began at her heart, the old cry came again to her lips, " Mother, sweetest mother, come back to me."

Of all the children who came to sit or play with Violet, she loved Fritz Adler the best. He and his little sister Ella were her almost daily visitors. Fritz's mother, the baker's wife opposite, always complained that Fritz was the " wildest fly " in all the town ; and there certainly appeared to be an unusual amount of life about him, but perhaps this was just what made his company so pleasant to her. He always brought into her room a bright face and a hearty laugh, a great rush of free joyousness, which seemed to lift the heart of the sick child out of its languor and make it beat for the time healthily and happily.

Besides this, she had trust in Fritz. He had never told her a lie, and she relied implicitly on all he said to her. With his curling hair and his bright eyes, his fresh colour and his careless stride, he was the very embryo of a young German soldier, prepared to conquer or to die, and fear had no place in his heart.

A greater contrast than he presented to poor little Violet could not be imagined. She was so still, so pale, so passive. Her eyes, instead of sparkling, were grave, large, and almost the colour of her violet dress ; and since her mother's death Fritz was almost the only person who had succeeded in making her laugh outright, and even this had been on very rare occa- sions.

Ella, like her brother, was the very personification of rude health. She had rosy cheeks, curly fair hair which hung over her shoulders, dimpled hands, and great sturdy legs. She was simply Fritz's shadow. He exercised the same curious influence over her which he did over Violet. When Fritz galloped up and down the street, sword in hand, threatening death to every Frenchman who ever breathed, Ella was sure to be following behind him as fast as her fat legs would allow, imitating his every word and gesture. When Fritz fell unexpectedly into the gutter, Ella was certain to fall on the top of him ; when Fritz sat in his little wooden cart drawn by Nero, the great black Newfoundland, and rushed down the cobbled hill at full speed, Ella was invariably beside him, with her fair hair floating out behind her in a yellow halo, and her fat legs propped on the little wooden board in front of her.

If there was one thing more than another that Violet longed to be able to do, it was to drive in this cart. When she saw the wooden box flying down the street past the window, with the children seated in it, her heart gave great leaps of excitement, and she leaned almost dangerously forward in her chair to see them reach the foot of the hill. But the coming home was somewhat more tedious. Nero was very good at galloping down hill, but exceedingly bad about coming up it again. Fritz generally urged him forward on these occasions by stout tugs at his tail and fearful guttural sounds, in which Ella joined until her very cheeks grew purple ; but Nero had evidently not a sensitive tail, and when toiling up the hill he seemed also to grow quite deaf.

It tired Violet to watch them returning; for when she heard Fritz's excited adjurations, and saw Ella's cheeks blown out like a roasted apple, she felt somehow as if she were drawing the carriage up the hill herself; and her shoulders used to ache so that she had to give up looking out of the window, and lean back in her chair.

Violet had a little basket fastened to a cord, which she could let down into the street from her window, and into which the children and the neighbours were in the habit of putting little presents. The baker's wife, Fritz's mother, often ran across the street and put in gingerbread cakes, still warm from the oven. The confectioner's boy, too, as he went by with his loaded tray of dainties, had a commission from his master to drop a package of sugar almonds or other sweets into the little wicker-work basket. Fritz, also, who was ingenious, had contrived an arrangement by which a little bell could be rung from the street up into her little turret-window whenever there was a gift waiting below for her in the street. But Fritz was also exceedingly mischievous; and one day, when he had rung the bell somewhat violently, and Violet had let down her small basket, she had found inside when she opened it only a large yellow frog squatting on a vine leaf, which immediately leaped out, first on her purple dress, and then upon the floor, where the cat pounced on it, and Violet's screams rang through the house. But Fritz had already reached the door, and the frog was carried off in his red pocket-hand-kerchief, and replaced among the cabbages in the back garden.

After this she always opened her basket cautiously, especially when the bell was rung with unusual vio-lence. And on one occasion, observing the legs of a cockroach issuing from the wicker sides of the basket, she opened the lid with special care, and seeing its contents, she turned the basket upside down, and shook everything quickly into the street beneath. The punishment was complete; for Fritz, who was standing directly underneath and gaping upwards, received a perfect shower of cockroaches on his face; and little Ella, also, who was smilingly gazing up at the window, had to rush into the shop opposite, to her mother, to have some of the struggling black creatures released from her web of yellow hair.

This was one of the occasions on which Violet had really laughed. It would have been impossible not to do so, as the mirth which rose up from the street beneath was infectious to the last degree. Fritz's father, standing at his door, and over whose head clouds of steam were issuing from the bakery beyond,

laughed at his son's discomfiture till the tears ran
down his cheeks; and even the grim policeman walked
out into the middle of the street, partly to avoid the
black insects which were swarming on the narrow
pavement beneath, and partly to catch a sight of little
Violet's face.   He had heard her laugh, and it had
sounded like music in his ears; but now, as she
glanced out quickly, he walked on again with a steady
tread and a face like iron.   His sword clanked against
the pavement, and the spike on his helmet shone
severely bright, and none could guess, as he passed
them, that the heart so tightly fastened up within his
blue uniform was soft as the baker's dough in the
shop beside him, or that his eyes were blinded at this
very moment with sudden tears.

There were occasions when even he had placed
gifts in the basket;—little toys which other hands had
played with; story books which other eyes had feasted
on greedily, and on whose pages were the marks of
the little fingers which had held them once, so tightly
and eagerly grasped; and occasionally a bundle of
snowdrops had been dropped in hastily, whose stalks
had been rolled in damp moss to keep them fresh till
the morning, for he always placed his gifts in the
basket at night-time.   He rang no bell; no eye saw
him.   He did not call out to the little figure seated

in the window above, with the shaded lamp burning
on the table beside her ; he asked for no thanks, but
passed on with the same official tread, the same
clanking sword, and the same ache for ever at his
heart.

Violet never knew who it was that placed these
presents in her basket. She often asked Fritz if he
could guess ; but though he did guess the butcher, the
chestnut-seller, and the lamplighter, simply because
they had children, he never thought of the grave
policeman, who so often, as he walked past, threatened
to put him in prison.

Violet treasured these gifts more than all her other
presents. She felt, by a kind of instinct, that there
was some story connected with them. On the fly-
leaf of one book she had read with a sudden sting of
strongest pain these words,—" For my own sick
girlie, from her little mother."

" Her little mother !" She had gazed at the crabbed
characters till this word seemed to rise up off the page
and enter into her very heart ; immense tears gathered
in her eyes, and fell in stars of bitterness upon the
paper,—" For my own sick girlie, from her little
mother."

In the evening she had said to Fritz in a low voice,
almost imploring in its entreaty,—

"Couldst not thou, dear Fritz, find out for me who gave me this?"

"I have told thee already," replied Fritz, who was busy sharpening a wooden sword on the hard edge of the lowest window-sill. "It is the lamplighter; I am certain of it. Whenever he goes by with his ladder and lantern, I remark he is always looking up at this house and at thee; and, besides, his pockets are always bulged out as if he had heaps of things in them."

The reasoning was, no doubt, good; but it did not satisfy Violet.

"But has he any children, Fritz?" she asked softly and a little doubtfully, for Fritz sometimes grew impatient if his words were questioned.

"Of course he has—hundreds of them."

"But are any of them sick — sick, I mean, like me?" she pleaded anxiously.

"Sick like thee?" he repeated vaguely, for his mind was still engrossed entirely with sharpening the deadly blade which he held in his hand; which he did by moistening it in his mouth and rubbing it on the wood before him, so that the window-sill was now quite black with paint, and so were his lips—"Sick like thee? How can I tell? All I know is, he has only one child, and she is the greatest goose in all the town—that fat red-haired girl called Minna, who sits under the red umbrella on the steps of the chapel and sells fruit."

Violet shook her head and sighed. Fritz's description of the lamplighter's daughter did not fit in with her thoughts at all. The little sick maiden reading the book given her by her mother did not resemble in any point Fritz's fat girl selling fruit on the chapel steps.

Again she sighed heavily, and murmured to herself, half in a whisper, " Oh, I wonder ! "

" What do you wonder about ? What do you want to know ? I'll tell you if you don't bother," said Fritz quickly.

" I want to know if Minna could ever have had a ' little mother.' "

Fritz had by this time succeeded in smashing the blade of the sword short off close to the very handle, and was standing up now, looking very red and angry opposite her, with a fearful smudge of paint on his lip and another on his cheek.

" Violet ! " he cried passionately, " see what thou hast made me do ! Thou art a little goose thyself." He waved the broken stump of the sword in his hand, and then he stopped.

Violet's book had slipped off her knees on to the floor,

and Fritz, with his natural rough politeness, had stooped to pick it up. As he did so, he saw the written inscription on the fly-leaf. For a full minute he gazed at it; then looking up covertly at her, he saw that she had tears in her eyes.

"Violet," he cried remorsefully, with his two stout arms stretched out to embrace and comfort her, "don't cry; it could not be the same girl, for," he added with decision, "Minna never had any mother; of that I am quite sure."

CHAPTER V.

A STRANGE BOOK.

THAT evening, when John returned from the forest, he found his little daughter flushed and excited, with her eyes shining purple in the twilight and a strange earnestness in her manner, which, he feared, spoke of a sudden uprising of fever,—that fever which was so slowly but surely wasting away her little life.

"Thou hast not been very long by thyself, hast thou, my sweet one?" he said anxiously, as he looked at the eyes raised up so lovingly to his, but still full of some strange and hidden tremor.

"Oh no, Fritz has been here; and, besides, I have been reading." She glanced with almost the nervousness of guilt at the little table beside her, and moved herself restlessly on her chair.

"My darling has been tiring herself, I fear," said John, sitting down on the window-sill beside her, and putting his great arm round her lovingly. "Well, now that father is returned, dost thou know—canst

thou guess what he has been about all the afternoon?"

"No, father," she said softly, laying her head down
on his shoulder with a long, weary breath. Her
thoughts were evidently engrossed by some subject of
which he knew nothing.

"Ah, my sweet one must not sigh like that," he
said, drawing her tenderly towards him; "it makes
father's heart ache; and, besides, when Violet hears
father's news, instead of crying, she will almost fly
out of her chair with joy."

"What!" she cried, sitting so suddenly up that
John was almost terrified, and had to loose his close
grasp of his little girl; "tell me, father, quickly,
quickly, tell Violet thy news."

John gazed at her in silent wonder. He did not
understand this mood—the brightly-glittering eyes,
the deepening flush, the expression of a burning but
unspoken anxiety, and the constant restless motion
of the little hand which lay hot and dry in his
palm.

"What hast thou been reading?" he asked curiously,
stretching out his arm towards the little table beside
her, on which now for the first time he had noticed a
book—a strange book with a yellow-spotted paper
cover and red edges. It was open, but was turned

down upon the Bible which always rested on the
table beside her chair—her mother's Bible, the most
precious thing she had in all the world.

" Who gave thee this new book, and what story
hast thou been troubling thy poor head with ? " he
asked kindly, as he would have lifted it from its
resting-place.

" Ah, do not touch it," she cried quickly,. as she
withdrew one hand from his grasp and laid it on the
yellow-spotted cover; " I have not finished it yet.
It is too lovely a story, and—first—first I must tell
it all to Fritz; and then—then, father, if Fritz says it
is true, then I will tell it all to thee." She ended
her sentence with a quick sob of excitement.

" Who gave thee the book, Violet ? "

" I do not know, father." She rubbed her fingers
up and down the cover restlessly.

" Thou dost not know ? "

" No ; I have tried to think, but cannot tell. Fritz
said perhaps it was the lantern-man gave it to me;
but then his girl never had any mother."

" My little life, my heart's blood, what ails thee ?
Let us talk no more of books or lantern-men, but
instead, we will speak of the grand carriage that
father is going to make for his Violet," cried John,
beside himself with a sudden fear that the fever had

risen to the sick child's head, and was filling the poor, weary brain with distracting fancies.

He lifted her out of her chair with tenderest love, and, sitting down by the stove, all forgetful of the evening meal which he so much needed after his day's work, he told her, in quiet, unexcited tones, as he rocked her gently to and fro on his knee, how all the week he had been thinking over a design of a little carriage which he was going to make for her, and for which he had gone that afternoon to the forest to choose wood—a carriage with springs, which could go over the cobbles outside and not shake her poor back, and into which her pillows could all be put, and in which she would be as comfortably propped up as if she were in her chair at home. "And if that does not succeed, and my little one is too tired to drive, then we shall make a carriage with handles to it, and we shall carry thee everywhere thou choosest to go. Fritz and I can take thee out on Sundays for long drives. Is it not so, Violet?"

"Yes, thou and Fritz," she echoed softly; "and then I can go down the hill and see the place where mother is asleep; cannot I, father?"

"Yes, my heart, we will go there first."

"Will she know I am there? Is she too far up, father?"

" I cannot tell, darling."

" But if—if—if Violet had—"

The question died on her lips, and John had become strangely silent. By-and-by, as the room darkened and the long summer evening grew shadowy, he rose up and lifted his little weary daughter in his arms and laid her down on her bed. This time the knots came undone without trouble, and no Kate was needed to assist in putting on the white frilled night-dress, or to shake up the pillows behind her aching shoulders. John seemed to-night to have hands like her mother's, so softly did he lay her down and so quietly did he sit by her side stroking her hair while she said the prayers her mother had taught her, and to which her little lips remained ever faithful. As he leaned over her to give her his good-night and a kiss, she said softly, "Another kiss, father;" which having received, she murmured to herself lovingly, " Good-night, father ; good-night, mother ; " and soon she was fast asleep.

CHAPTER VI.

GREAT EXCITEMENT.

WHEN John knew by Violet's regular breathing that she was fast asleep, he rose gently from his seat beside the bed and went over to the little table, on which lay, amongst so many others of the child's treasures, the mother's Bible and the gold-spotted book.

He took them up with quite a reverent, almost a guilty touch, and placed them with care upon the larger table at the foot of the bed. Then he lit the lamp, shaded it, and having once more leaned over the bed to see that Violet slept, he sat down to look at this new book in the pretty paper cover which seemed by its contents to have so excited and interested her.

He placed his finger in the page at which he found it open, and turned first to look at the title. He smiled rather sadly as he read the name, for it was a book that he remembered well having read himself when he was a youngster. He had forgotten the stories now, but he recognized the clumsy woodcut which had had the power not so long ago to thrill his own heart with a feverish excitement, and make it beat with a mixed enthusiasm and distress.

But it was with no mixed distress that his eye fell on the page where he had just placed his finger, and which had evidently been the centre point of poor little Violet's interest. On one side of the open book was a plate, divided by the old-fashioned style into three consecutive pictures, one above, one in the middle, and one at the foot of the page. On the opposite side was a short poem, consisting of three verses, each verse explanatory of the plate opposite it.

It was called "The Hunchbacked Girl;" and as his eyes fell on the name and the pictures which accompanied it, he closed the book hurriedly, and said in a voice straining between anger and tears, "How wicked! They shall answer to me for this."

But by-and-by, making a strong effort over himself, he opened at the page again and stared at the plates and the print until he saw them no more.

The first picture represented a woman lying, evidently at the verge of death, in one of the garret rooms of a house situated in a large town; for one could see through the open window the roofs of houses opposite and the top of a church steeple. By

her side knelt a man with a child in his arms, which
he was holding up towards its mother to receive from
her a last embrace ; for her hands were outstretched
also : and underneath were written the words, " Auf
wiedersehen " (To meet again).

The second picture represented a little child propped
up in a chair at the same window, with its head
resting on its hand and its eyes looking out deso-
lately across the roofs and the steeple to the sky
beyond. Underneath, in small text, were printed
these two words, pathetic in their simplicity, " Ganz
allein " (All alone).

In the third picture the room was the same, but
the chair stood empty at the window. The little
pallet in the corner was empty also ; but in the
centre of the apartment, with eyes steadfastly uplifted, and with a radiant smile upon its face, stood
the little hunchbacked child. On either side was an
angel, holding it by its hands ; and from between its
poor, weary shoulders had sprung up two shining
wings, rising into the air behind it, and apparently
stretching themselves out for flight. Underneath
was written, in the same small, close, old-fashioned
printing, " Keine thräne mehr " (No more tears).

John did not trust himself to look at the story.
He laid his face down on the page and stretched out

his hand on the table, while his fingers closed tightly on his palm.

"God help my little Violet," he said bitterly to himself; "as long as I live she shall never be left alone."

But even as he spoke, while his head was still bowed over the open page before him, and his heart throbbed heavily against the wooden table, he was aware of an unusual stir in the street beneath, a hum of voices rising higher and higher, the trampling of many feet, and far off, near the barrack square, a bugle call, loud and shrill, which made him start up from his sitting posture and walk quickly to the window.

But what a sight it was his eyes fell upon! The street, so silent and peaceful a few minutes ago, and to all intents and purposes empty, was now a surging mass of human beings. All Edelsheim seemed gathered together in this one narrow thoroughfare. Every moment the voices were becoming louder, the excitement greater. It was with difficulty the lamp-lighter could force his way through the crowd to light the large lamp which hung in the centre of the street on a chain suspended across the roadway from the Adlers' house to his own.

John opened the window for a moment, and looked

out across the wooden box filled with violets which
stood in the old mullioned embrasure.

"Hist," he cried, leaning down and trying to catch
the attention of some one immediately beneath the
window, " what has happened ? "

The question was heard, for a woman looking
suddenly upwards to see who spoke, flung her arms
high up into the air and cried out in a shrilly voice
of anguish, "War is proclaimed."

He closed the window as suddenly as he had opened
it, gave one glance towards the little bed to see that
Violet was still asleep, and then sank down upon the
broad window seat with his face covered.

War is proclaimed!　Only three words, and yet
the whole town was already rocking with their
import.　Bells were ringing, shouts were rising, men
and women stood so closely packed beneath that one
could have walked across their heads with safety.
Exultant youths, full of their young life and young
blood, so soon to be given and spilt for God and
Fatherland, were flinging their caps in the air ; men,
too, with beards and grizzled hair, shouted and gestic-
ulated frantically ; others, grave and silent, turned
their voices inward and cried aloud to the God of the
fatherless and widow.　Fritz, in his night-dress, at
the little gable window opposite, was blowing a shrill

tin trumpet and screaming out, in his high, boyish voice, "War, war, war!" which was echoed by a still higher treble in the room beyond.

At last Violet stirred. It was almost impossible that with such a din going on outside she could sleep on.

In a moment John had risen and was kneeling at her bedside. His hand had clasped the little fingers which lay so loosely upon the knitted counterpane. His bearded cheek was close to the white face on the pillow, barely discernible now in the closely-shaded light of the lamp which burned at the foot of the bed. He was ready with the word of love to quiet her alarms, and with a kiss to soothe her back to sleep, but they were not needed. She merely moved restlessly to and fro on her pillow, and muttered to herself in some dreamful excitement,—

"Look! look out into the street! What dost thou see, father?"

John bent low over the child's face and touched it gently with his lips. He must have kissed her then, or his heart would have broken.

Even in her sleep Violet knew who was bending over her. "Father," she said softly.

"Yes, my heart's love, I am here beside thee."

"Seest thou? is it not lovely?"

" What ? what ? " he asked with a sob.

" The little hunchback has wings."

After this she gave a long, restful sigh, and turned her head against her father's arm. Nor did the noise in the street disturb her any more, though the cries at times rose almost to shrieks, and though the lamp in her room burned on unextinguished until daylight had taken its place.

CHAPTER VII.

FRITZ AND ELLA.

THE next day there seemed little if any diminution of
the excitement. The crowd was not quite so dense;
but ordinary business appeared for the time almost
suspended. People were rushing up and down the
street with slips of paper in their hands on which
were printed the latest telegrams; and persons who
were usually engrossed with their work in the early
hours of the day were standing at the doors of their
shops and houses discussing the great news of impend-
ing war, news which gathered with every hour fresh
confirmation.

Violet, of course, seated as usual in her chair in the
window, could not but notice the bustle and the stir
beneath; but it did not frighten or distress her, for
her father had brought his work up to her room quite
early this morning, and when he was near her she
always reposed on his strength and courage in place
of her own.

But John was both distressed and disturbed; and presently seeing that Violet's hair was a little blown about by the wind, he made it a pretext for closing over the casement, so that she might not hear what the people were talking about so earnestly in the street underneath; and for a time his efforts were successful.

It was only as the day wore on and it came near the time when he had to go to the store for orders that she grew restless, and the anxious pleading look came into her eyes which he never could bear to see, and which to-day he felt less able than ever to withstand.

" I shall not be long away, darling," he said softly as he gathered up his tools and laid them on the broad window-sill beside her. " See, I am not taking away my work materials, and I shall be back almost before thou thinkest that I am gone. I will send Kate to sit with thee, and thou canst teach her how to paint the ducks for the magnet-box, only this time I would not give them scarlet wings; black, I think, would be better."

Violet smiled at the idea of Kate's trying to paint the ducks—Kate, who was so blind that she could not see a cockroach creeping across the kitchen floor, and the length of whose nails would sadly interfere with her holding the paint-brush.

"I would rather have Fritz to sit with me," she said plaintively.

"Fritz! ah, well; but is not this the time for his school?"

"He has not been at school all to-day. I have seen him ever so often at the window. See, father, he is there now; and oh! only look what a dress he has got on."

She burst out laughing, and even John with his heavy heart could not repress a smile, for there at the window opposite stood Fritz with an enormous spiked helmet on his head; a huge military coat buttoned across his chest, which covered his whole body; and a pair of riding-boots on his legs, which evidently encumbered him a good deal, for just at this moment, while John and Violet were gazing at him, he made a sudden rush at some unseen enemy beside the curtain, and one of the boots doubling up at the ankle he fell waddling on the floor, his helmet tumbling off his head and going almost out of the window, while all his efforts to get up again, even with the assistance of fat Ella, who tugged at him with all her might and main, were fruitless.

Again Violet burst out into one of those rare fits of real childlike laughter which always delighted and refreshed poor John's heart; but to-day, though he

smiled somewhat grimly, he turned away quickly to
the door, saying as he went: " I shall see about Fritz
coming to sit with thee; but if his mother will not
permit it thou must be content for awhile with Kate."

"Yes, yes," cried Violet after him; "but do, please,
send Fritz here. I have something so particular to
ask him."

She watched her father as he crossed over the street
to the baker's. He was such a great tall man that he
had generally to stoop as he went in at the doorway;
but to-day Madam Adler met him at the entrance to
the bakery, and they held what seemed to the watcher
at the window upstairs a very lengthy conversation.
Madam Adler, who was a round fat little body,
gesticulating somewhat wildly, pointed first up the
street and then down it, and clutched every now and
then at her cap, which was hanging half off the back
of her head, while she gazed up at the great tall man
beside her, whose grave eyes were fixed intently upon
her face, and who listened earnestly while she poured
forth a torrent of words, not one of which Violet could
hear from the buzz and noise in the street beneath.

Fritz, who had regained his legs by this time, was
now standing in the window opposite, making frantic
signs across to Violet, who at first remained quite
unconscious of his efforts; but presently looking up

she saw him waving a sword furiously across the
street to attract her attention; and seeing now he
had secured it, he proceeded to make a sudden lunge
at Ella, digging the weapon apparently deep into the
very middle of her body. Ella immediately collapsed
on the floor, and Fritz continued for some time to
prod her violently. Violet screamed and turned away
her head; but when she looked round again, Ella, with
an enormous brown paper helmet on her head, was
standing beside Fritz in the very middle of the window
grinning from ear to ear, while her assailant, still
martially attired in the old trailing coat, and with a
face flushed with victory, had his arm thrown affectionately round her neck.

By-and-by, as Violet still gazed across and smiled
more and more at Fritz's excited movements, she saw
her father enter the room opposite. He sat down in
a chair a little distance from the window and called
Fritz over to him, and a conversation ensued apparently of some interest, as Fritz never lifted his eyes
from John's face while he was speaking to him, and
Ella's countenance also assumed a kind of rigid
stolidity most unnatural to it.

But this tranquillity did not last long; for no sooner
had John left the room, having shaken hands with
Fritz and kissed Ella, than a kind of secondary excite-

ment seemed to take possession of the children. Fritz
first took off his own helmet, and then, while Ella was
stooping down to unloosen her brown paper leggings,
he snapped hers off also with a summary politeness
which Ella seemed for a moment to resent; but Fritz
had no time, evidently, to give to trifles. He laid both
helmets on the foot of a couch which projected out
into the window, and then he rapidly divested himself
of his coat and his huge leather boots, winding up by
planting Ella on the end of the sofa and tugging
violently at her less cumbersome leggings, until the
little girl descended suddenly upon her back on the
floor.

This time a few tears evidently softened the heart
of the warrior, for he stooped down, lifted Ella from
the ground, and covered her face with kisses; and in a
few minutes Violet saw them both emerge from their
house hand-in-hand and cross over the street, and
push through the gathering of people towards the door
of her own house, which opened immediately beneath
her window.

She felt rather sorry that Ella had come across with
her brother, for she had something to say to Fritz, a
question to ask him in secret about some subject which
was troubling her, and which she felt she could only
confide to him in private. But when the door of her

room opened and Ella burst in all smiles and health and happiness, and rushed over to fling her dimpled arms round Violet's neck, she forgot for a time about her secret; and her spirits rose, and her white face broke into one of its sudden smiles, as she noticed scraps of cord and paper still sticking to Ella's fat legs which Fritz had evidently been too hurried to remove.

"What hast thou been doing all this morning, Ella?" she asked curiously; "and why has Fritz not been at school? I have seen him ever since I was dressed, playing in the window."

Ella's cheeks suddenly deepened to a purple red, and she gazed towards her brother with eyes which said plainly, "Thou must give an answer to this question."

"I have not been at school because—because, well, because I did not go; and besides I was busy doing lots of other things."

Ella's face looked decidedly relieved by this explanation of her brother's, which was entirely satisfactory to her own mind; but Violet was much puzzled by Fritz's words and still more perplexed by his manner, which was strange and quite unlike himself.

While she was pondering with herself what it all meant Ella broke in upon the silence.

" Yes, Fritz was doing lots of things all the morning—killing and cutting and stabbing the French, and he gave me an awful scrape on the arm; just look at it, Violet !" And Ella turned round the fattest of arms to Violet for compassionate inspection, across which just at the pink and dimpled elbow there certainly was a most undeniable and somewhat gory scratch.

" Hold thy tongue, thou little gabbling goose of a chatterbox," cried Fritz, turning suddenly round in real anger and casting a glance of withering scorn upon his unhappy sister ; " hast thou already forgotten what I said to thee in the hall downstairs ?"

" I did not say anything about the war," said Ella in reply, covering her face suddenly with her frilled pinafore and grasping on to the side of the invalid's chair, while she stretched out her hand as if to defend herself ;—" I did not say one word about the war, did I, Violet ?"

" No, no ; she said nothing—nothing that I heard. She is a good little lamb, and thou must not frighten her, Fritz," cried Violet soothingly, as she drew the little sobbing girl over to her side and held her arm tightly round her fat waist.

" She is a good little new-born donkey," snorted Fritz still in much virtuous anger ; " she has no more

sense than the head of a pin. I told her something
only a moment ago downstairs, and the instant she
gets up into the room she must begin to let out the
whole secret."

" What secret ?"

" About the war," sobbed Ella.

" About what war ? I do not understand. Why is
it a secret, and why should Ella not tell me ?" she
added in a distressed voice.

" He said if I did tell thee he would cut my tongue
out with his sword, and give me to the policeman to
put me into the prison," sobbed Ella.

" For shame, Fritz ! how couldst thou frighten her
so ?" said Violet with quite a hot flush on her usually
pale face.—" I will not let him touch thee, Ella.
There, put down thy apron ; Fritz was only laughing
at thee."

" Of course," cried Fritz contemptuously ; " but she
is such a little thrush, she would swallow a camel,
hump and all, if one only held it up to her mouth."

This brilliant sally was suggested by the descent
of one of Violet's newly-painted animals upon Fritz's
head from the window-ledge above.

" I would not swallow a camel—I am not a thrush,"
still sobbed Ella, hiding her face against Violet's chair.

" Well, well, what does it signify ? stop crying,"

cried Fritz, making an effort over himself to recover
his usual gallantry. "Come along, let's have some
fun.—May we take down all those old beasts overhead and have a game with them ?—may we, Violet ?
We have not played at crossing the desert for ages."

"Yes, yes; only take care. Some of them are
quite sticky, and one or two have broken legs; but
there are lots of other animals in the Noah's ark in
the corner."

"All right; now we shall have real good fun," cried
Fritz, tugging Ella's lingering arm from the rungs of
Violet's chair with reassuring roughness and making
room for her on the bench beside him. "Now, thou
shalt be Noah, and Violet shall be Aaron, and I will
be Moses with the rod."

"What rod ?" asked Ella, gazing up at her brother
rather doubtfully with eyes all wet and smudged with
tears, while she wriggled herself into a more comfortable position on the carpenter's hard bench beside
him.

"Oh, not the rod thou meanest," he replied reassuringly as he emptied out pell-mell a whole box full of
animals upon the table—cows, sheep, ducks, elephants,
and canary birds, all heaped up in a mound of wild
confusion.

Ella had by this time her yellow curly head

pillowed confidingly against Fritz's left shoulder, and perfect harmony was restored between them. Violet was now the most silent of the three. For some minutes past she had seemed in a reverie, and occasionally she looked anxiously across at Fritz, as if longing but fearing to ask him some question.

Whether he was aware of these longing, sorrowful glances directed towards him, it was impossible to tell. One might perhaps have thought so from the way he rambled on in a foolish, disconnected style, while he ranged the animals two by two along the edge of the table, and elicited shrieks of laughter from Ella by making the broken-legged elephant sit on its tail, while the no-legged goose was given a lift across the desert, seated between the horns of a scarlet cow.

At last they were all arranged in order, from the elephant down to the little red spotted lady-bird, which was fully as large as the mouse some distance in front of it; and Ella was desired to keep her feet and arms under the table, as every time she stretched them out she was certain to overturn a whole cavalcade of animals.

"Now Moses is going to drive them all into the ark, and I am Moses," cried Fritz triumphantly; "and any that are stupid and won't go in for me, Aaron

can pick up and push them in after Moses, as hard as
he likes."

"But Moses did not drive the animals into the
ark, nor Aaron either," said Violet smiling.

"Yes, yes," shouted Ella, kicking her toes against
the underneath part of the table, so that several of
the astonished animals suddenly leaped high into the
air and then fell down on their sides—"yes, yes;
Fritz is right. Moses drove them in, every one, into
the ark; he whacked them with his rod, and off they
galloped."

"For shame, Ella!" cried Violet, though she could
not help laughing a little as she looked at the joyous
round face opposite her, stretched in innocent smiles
from ear to ear; "it was Noah who drove the animals
into the ark; and besides, that story is in the Bible."

"But Fritz said it was Moses," repeated Ella,
whose confidence in Fritz's veracity was not easily to
be shaken.

"I know I did, but I was wrong. It was Noah of
course—only, what does it matter? I never can remember the names of those very old men; and besides
I don't much care for Bible stories—I like bits of
them, that's all."

"Oh!" said Violet, with a sound of such unmistakable dismay in her voice that Fritz looked up

surprised; "thou dost not care for Bible stories, Fritz ?"

"No, he does not; only bits—bits the size of a crumb," chimed in Ella, who was busy crushing the heads of two stags together, to the total destruction of their antlers.

. "Hold thy tongue, Ella," cried Fritz angrily; "I do like some Bible stories, of course : Daniel in the lions' den; and Gehazi, who was turned white for telling a lie—that's a grand story; and the little child who was standing in the corn in the sun and got a headache, and who was made alive after he was dead, and given back to his mother—I like that best of all."

"So do I," screamed Ella, whose mirth was momentarily becoming more irrepressible. "Get in, old humpy back, into thy box; get in, I say, old beast." This speech was addressed to a kind of violet-coloured camel which had stuck in the entrance to the ark and was now standing head downwards amongst its imprisoned comrades with its heels elevated in the air.

"Ella, thou great goose, thou stupid little child, what art thou saying ? thou must not speak of humps to Violet." A sudden push from Fritz's elbow sent the astonished Ella rolling off the bench on to the floor.

"Violet," cried Fritz, suddenly looking up and

taking no notice whatever of his sister's descent, for at this moment a spasm of recollection had flashed across his mind, " dost thou know, Violet, the lamplighter's girl *has* a mother ? I saw her yesterday morning in the market selling fish."

" Selling fish ? " said Violet, repeating Fritz's words in a curious, absent manner.

" Yes ; and such an old lobster I never saw. Her hands were just like claws, and—but what is the matter with thee ? why art thou crying ? It is all the fault of that horrid little Ella. But never mind ; mother slapped me for speaking about thy hump, and Ella shall get slapped too."

" I am not crying," said Violet, vainly trying to keep back a sob; " it is only because I have been waiting so long, Fritz, to say something to thee."

" Not about the war ? " cried Fritz, colouring crimson and bending his face down suddenly on the table. " I promised thy father I would tell thee nothing about it."

" It is nothing about war. It is a secret, but —but I could not say it to thee before Ella ; she would not understand."

" Well, Ella shall go.— Come along home, thou little good-for-nought, and I will carry thee across on my back."

Ella at these words half moved out from her hiding-place under the wooden table, whither after her fall she had retreated in some dudgeon, but she almost immediately drew herself in again, and said flatly,—

"Ella will not go home; mother will smack her for calling the camel a—"

"Hist, thou little goose; mother will do nothing of the kind. Get up quickly, or I will not carry thee at all; there, hold on tightly now and keep thy heels quiet, for it is getting so dark and the stairs are so narrow I might fall down and break thy neck. Say good-evening now to Violet, and away we go."

He carried Ella over to Violet's chair, and the little maiden put her soft loving arms about her neck and kissed her with all the strength of her childish heart.

"Ella did not make thee cry, Violet, did she? Ella did not know that thou wast so fond of the poor—" She did not finish her sentence, for Fritz whirled her away suddenly.

But Violet called down the stairs after her, "Ella did not make Violet cry; Ella is a good girl. Good-evening, sweet Ella."

It was almost dusk when Fritz returned, and John had not yet come home. Violet heard the boy's step on the stairs, and her heart beat so fast that the neck of her little purple frock heaved up and down flutteringly.

She had packed away all the animals she could fit into the Noah's ark, and the others she had placed in a heap on the window-sill. There was nothing now on the table before her but her mother's Bible and the book with the gold-spotted cover.

For the twentieth time since Fritz had left the room, she had opened this book at the picture of the little hunchback and as hastily closed it again. " I will ask him first, and then I will show it to him," she said in a whisper to herself as she looked up nervously at the opening door.

But Fritz came in quite unconscious of the flutter-ing heart; his own was beating so hard that he had to sit down on the chair by the stove to get his breath, and it was some moments before he gasped,—

" Well, if ever I take that great fat Ella on my back again! I would rather carry a cow to market on my shoulders than have her hanging on to my neck and throttling me. First she made me carry her up to the top of the house, to the very garret, because she said mother was there; and then all the way down again, because she said mother was in the bake-house. Then I had to haul her all the way off again down the street to Madame Bellard's, and up to the

top of that house, where we found mother and
Madame Bellard crying over their coffee like two
sea-crabs; and there I left Ella gaping at them with
her eyes nearly falling out on her cheeks. Pah! she
weighs at the least three tons."

"What were they crying about?" asked Violet
curiously; "I saw so many people crying in the street
to-day."

"People often cry when they have nothing else to
do," he said, jumping up suddenly from his chair and
raking out the ashes from the stove vehemently,—"at
least Ella does; but of course they had something to cry
for—only it is a secret, and thou must not ask me."

"A secret?" she said, nervously pushing the little
book in front of her up and down the table. "Thou
hast not asked me yet, Fritz, what my secret is."

"What is it, then?" he asked, coming close up to
the table; and then recognizing the gold-spotted cover
on the back of which Violet's fingers were trembling
visibly, he added, "Is it about the lamplighter's girl?
or hast thou perhaps found out the name of the little
mother?"

"No," said Violet, shaking her head; "I cannot
think who the mother is. But oh, there is such a
lovely story in her book, Fritz, and I want so much
to ask of thee, 'Is it true?'"

"Show it to me," said Fritz cheerfully. "Of course I can tell it to thee at once."

But Violet covered the book with both her hands; and though it was now almost dusk, he noticed how the blood rushed over her white face, and she looked for a little while out of the window.

"No, no—in a minute thou shalt see it; but first thou wilt tell me one thing, wilt thou not, Fritz? only one thing, but quite, quite truly;" and she turned her eyes upon him so earnestly that the boy felt almost frightened.

"Of course I will answer thee truly; but first I must hear thy question."

"If mother were here she could tell me all I want to know," sighed Violet, putting off the dreaded moment; "and father, I know he could also tell me, only he does not like me to talk about hunchbacks."

"About hunchbacks!" cried Fritz with a sudden gasp; "I do not know anything about hunchbacks."

"Yes, yes, thou dost," she cried excitedly. "I am a little hunchback; thou knowest that; thou saidst so thyself, Fritz, one day long ago. And now thou wilt tell me this one thing. Is it true—" She paused and breathed more quickly than ever; the question was evidently one of gigantic importance.

"Is what true?"

"That God gives the little hunchbacks these humps?"

"Yes, of course; that is to say, first they get a fall or something, and then God gives them the humps afterwards."

"And what does he put into them?"

"What? I do not understand thee."

"Is there not something inside of every poor hunchback's hump?"

"Yes, of course there is."

"Well, and what is it, Fritz? dear Fritz, tell me what it is." The question was breathed with actual pain.

"Dost thou mean what is in thy hump — this thing?" and Fritz laid his hand very softly on her shoulders.

"Yes."

"Why, any one knows that. Bones, of course; I can feel them."

"Bones?" she gasped.

"Yes; bones, and flesh, and skin, and all that kind of thing."

Violet's eyes distended; an anguish crept into them that appalled even Fritz. She drew the spotted book quickly over to her, and said slowly, as she opened it at the story of the hunchback, "Look at that picture,

Fritz: that little sick child had 'wings' in her hump, lovely silver wings; and are not books like this true, Fritz? There are angels in the page, and the little girl flies up to her mother, and people would not write what was not true about angels and—and heaven."

The question was a little puzzling; but Fritz answered it without hesitation.

" The stories in this book are all fairy tales. Look at the cover and thou canst see that for thyself."

" Fairy tales? but are fairy tales never true?"

" No; at least none that I ever read."

" But God, and the angels, and heaven are all in that book, and they are true; and the little sick hunchback, that is not a fairy tale, for I am sick just like her; and why—why must that one little bit be untrue? And besides," sobbed Violet, whose whole courage and hope seemed almost to have forsaken her, —" besides, the words under that picture are in the Bible. I found them in mother's own Bible: 'No more tears.'" As she lifted up her face to Fritz for some hope, some consolation, immense tears were running down her cheeks, and the boy felt a tightening in his own throat too.

" What does it matter?" he said as he pushed the spotted book away from her; " I will throw this

old thing out of the window if it makes thee cry.
Thou dost not want wings; thou art the best little
angel in all Edelsheim : and, besides, flies have wings,
and they are horrid beasts; and so why need one
care ?" and he threw his arms round her neck, and
kissed her wet face, and whispered every loving name
he could think of into her ear.

CHAPTER VIII.

THE next few days were so full of a new excitement
for Violet that she scarcely had time to think of the
little hunchback, or of the shock her feelings had received from Fritz's words.

All day long she sat in the window, absorbed in
watching what was going on in the street beneath.
Regiments of soldiers were constantly marching past,
bands were playing, and flags flying from many of the
opposite windows. Great forage-carts toiled up the
hill, driven by soldiers; and Uhlans were for ever dash-
ing up and down the street on their great tall horses,
so that the points of their lances often seemed to
come up to the very window at which she sat.

But Violet was not afraid of them, for even in
their haste they gave her often a nod as they went by.
Many of the Uhlans were friends of her father's, and
though she scarcely recognized some of them in their
square caps, they knew her; and not a few, as they

rode quickly past and saw the white face in the window, felt a shiver at their heart as they asked themselves the question, " If John goes to the war, what is to happen to the child ? "

But as yet the question was not decided, and though Violet had heard through Kate some talk of the war, her heart lay still in an unsuspecting calm.

Once, as she saw a little child crying in the street below and holding on to its father's long military coat in an anguish of grief, she lifted her head suddenly and said to her father, who was busy making one of the wheels for her new carriage, " Thou art not a soldier, father ? "

" No, darling, no, not at this moment."

" Thou wast a soldier once though, long ago, before Violet was born. Is it not so ? Fritz has told me thou wert."

" Yes, a long time ago."

" And wert thou ever in a battle, father ? "

" Yes, my sweetest treasure, in several; but we will not talk of battles. Thou hast not asked me all to-day about the carriage. I have got the springs home this morning from the blacksmith, and it will be so light when it is finished that even Fritz could draw thee about in it."

" How lovely to go up and down the street with

Fritz as Ella does, ever so fast down the hill, and ever so slow up. I am not so heavy as Ella, am I, father ?"

" No, my poor little daughter, I am afraid not."

" And thou, father, some day, thou wilt take me in my carriage to the hill, and we will gather nuts and bring them home in my carriage ; and every one will wonder when they see no one in the window. They will look up and they will say, 'Where is little Violet ?' and they will never think that she is gone far, far away, to that hill which is so very far off."

The child's face was radiant ; her eyes had turned to that deep purple hue which seemed always to match the shadows of her dress, and her cheeks had crimsoned with the thought of this new and wonderful life which was so soon to be hers.

Poor John put down his wheel and went over to his favourite seat on the broad sill beside her. He had purposely set her to talk on this theme, and now she was breaking his heart with her innocent raptures.

" I am afraid father is a great idler," he said, putting his head down very softly against her shoulder. " I ought to be downstairs in my workshop now, instead of chattering nonsense to thee all day."

" But we were not talking nonsense, were we,

father ? It is quite true about the carriage, is it not ? it is not a fairy tale, father ?"

" A fairy tale ?"

" Fritz says— ; " she paused.

" What does Fritz say ?" John asked the question somewhat dreamily. He had been gazing at her earnestly for some minutes, and now he kissed her twice passionately, as if without any apparent reason. " Thou art father's little treasure, his darling, his own sweet little maiden," he said with almost a sob in his throat, " and thou must try and grow strong for father's sake."

Violet looked up a little shyly, and put her arms round his neck. " And thou art the best father in all the world—dear, dear father."

The old policeman, walking by in the street, saw the little maiden with her arms so tightly clasped round her father's neck ; and he said to himself with a groan, " Poor maiden ! she knows it all now, and she would fain hold him back if she could ; " and he walked on.

But Violet did not know it all, nor for many days did the truth dawn upon her. It fell to Fritz's lot, as usual, to be the one to proclaim the tidings.

It was one evening about a month after war had been proclaimed. It had been a very hot day, and

Violet was tired and weak, and not inclined to play or talk. She was leaning back against her pillows looking out at the pigeons, which always came at this hour of a summer's afternoon to sit and preen their feathers on the lantern-chain which hung high up across the street.

She knew these pigeons quite well; she had given them all names. She placed crumbs for them every day on the window-sill beside her chair, and she delighted to see their fussy ways, twirling round and cooing angrily, and trying to push each other off the sill so as to secure the larger share of the food.

But to-day she only watched them languidly. For the last three days neither Fritz nor Ella had called in to play with her. She had seen them in the street hanging on to the backs of the forage-waggons, and Fritz had once appeared in the window opposite with Ella's doll speared at the end of a lance, but seeing Violet beckoning to him to come across, he had shaken his head lugubriously and disappeared from her sight.

So Violet, whose back was aching and whose little heart sank easily under any depressing influence, was alternately watching her father putting some finishing touches to the hood of her new carriage, and gazing out languidly at the pigeons and the storks on the red roofs, and the jackdaw in Fritz's window opposite, hopping everlastingly up and down from its perch, and screaming out some words which the baker's boy had taught it with much trouble to say.

Beyond the roofs and between the fretted spire of the church she saw also the hill, looking so green and fresh in the golden evening air; and above it there was a pale green sky, flecked with amber clouds and little bars of red.

Violet sighed heavily, and John looked up from his work.

" What ails my treasure ?"

" Nothing, father, only I am so, so tired; and Fritz and Ella, they have not come to see me for so many days."

" Ah, I will call over there presently and send them across to thee. I have but one or two nails to put in this hood, and then thy carriage will be finished; that is good, is it not ?"

" Delightful !" cried Violet, raising herself up in her chair to see better the last finishing touches put to her new possession ; but as she did so her eyes fell for a moment on the pavement opposite, where a soldier was just stopping at the Adlers' door with a bundle of papers in his hand, surrounded and followed by a large and excited crowd.

" What is it ? father, come here. There is such a
fuss in the street. A soldier has just gone in at the
Adlers' house, and all the people are standing at their
door, and one woman is crying."

" I am afraid a great many women and children
will cry before this evening is over," said her father
very gravely, as he rose and went over to the
window.

" Why, father ?"

" Because their husbands and fathers will have to
go away from them to the war, and leave them. Yes;
it is just as I thought. It is the orderly corporal
leaving the names at the different houses. Whose
turn will it be next ?"

" But Fritz's father cannot be sent to the war; he
is not a soldier, father ?"

" We must all be soldiers, little one, when a war
comes, and we are called out to fight."

" But thou, father, art not a soldier ; thou saidst so
to me thyself the other day. Father, dear father,
turn round thy face to me. Tell Violet that thou
wilt never be a soldier."

" I cannot tell Violet what she asks me," said John
slowly, turning his face and speaking in a strained,
thick voice. " If the king wants me to fight for God
and the Fatherland, of course I must go."

"But he does not want thee; he has not sent for thee?"

"Not yet," he said, sitting down beside his little girl, and lifting up one of her hands tenderly; "but he may want me. And if he does, I must go; must I not, Violet? Father could not stay at home if his king called him. A brave soldier is always ready to fight for his country."

"But thou art not a soldier, father. The king has not called; and if he were to call for thee, I would not let thee go. For if father goes away to the war, and leaves Violet all alone, she must die! she must die! she must die!" Violet sobbed, and rocked herself to and fro in her chair.

"There, there, my heart, thou must not say such things. The corporal has not called yet with father's name. Keep still, my lamb, and cease crying. Fritz will be here soon, and thou wilt see how brave he is. I will go over and call him," cried John, rising precipitately. The corporal had come out of the Adlers' house, and was crossing over towards their own doorway.

"Father, father, stay!" cried Violet. "I would rather have thee to sit with me than Fritz." She caught at his coat. "Come back to me! come back, come back!"

But he was already closing the door after him, and in a moment more she heard his footsteps hurrying down the stairs.

With eyes full of blinding tears, she turned quickly to see him emerge into the street beneath; but though she brushed them from her eyes, he was nowhere to be seen. She looked up at the windows opposite, but he was not there either—only she could see Fritz lying on his face on the floor, and Ella stooping caressingly over him, with her little white apron to her eyes.

The crowd was now gathered exactly under their own window, and Violet's heart beat so fast that at last she cried out loud in her misery, and Kate opening the door came in.

" Kate, Kate, where is father?" she cried out anxiously.

" Father is busy talking to the corporal downstairs. He cannot come up just yet."

" The corporal!" screamed Violet passionately; " he is not coming to call my father to the war? Go down, Kate, to the door, and tell him he must not call him away. Father could not go to the war and leave me all alone."

" No, no; to be sure not," said Kate soothingly. " Men with children have no business to go off fighting. I will tell him so when he comes up, and—

Ah, here comes Master Fritz, tearing across the street like a madman, and Miss Ella too."

"Shut the door!" screamed Violet. " I do not want to see Fritz; I do not want to see Ella: I want only father, only father to come back." But before Kate's stiff bones could bear her across the room, the door flew open and the children rushed in.

Fritz's cheeks were purple, his eyes were red, his blue-striped blouse was damp with tears. Ella tumbled in after him, her face also streaked and smeared from crying, and her pinafore hopelessly crumpled.

"Hast thou heard the news, Violet?" screamed Fritz excitedly. "The Reserve has been called out, and father is to go to the war !"

"What is the Reserve?"

"Oh, all the soldiers who have been out fighting before, long ago. My father was in lots of battles before, and so was yours."

"My father is not in the Reserve?" cried Violet, leaning forward eagerly.

"Yes; of course he is. I saw the corporal put the same blue paper into his hand downstairs as he did into father's a few minutes ago."

"And he is to go away to the war ?"

"Yes."

"When ?"

" The day after to-morrow."

Then such a cry of bitter anguish burst from Violet's lips that Fritz and Ella absolutely stood aghast with terror. She struggled wildly to get free from her chair, and to push her little table away which held her a close prisoner—" Let me out! let me down, Fritz, Ella ! I must find father.—Father, father, father !" till at last the bitter cry echoed through the room, the house, and out into the street.

Madam Adler opposite heard it, and thrust her fingers into her ears ; the policeman walking past covered his eyes suddenly with his gloved hands ; and John, saying farewell to the corporal in the hall, heard it also. In a few moments he was up the stairs, and held his darling close to his heart. Fritz and Ella speedily departed homewards, leaving the door wide open behind them. John rose and closed it, and he and Violet were left alone to their grief.

CHAPTER IX.

AUNT LIZZIE'S VISIT.

THE next day an aunt of Violet's arrived from a distant town. She was a sister of John's wife and a wife herself, very young and very fair, and with a wonderful likeness to the poor dead mother. Her husband, who was many years older than herself, was amongst the militia, and had not yet been called out; and at the cry from John's broken heart she came at once, leaving her own little ones behind her, to remain a few days with Violet, until the bitterness of the parting was over.

On this day the little girl had made no effort to leave her bed; all the long morning she had remained with her head buried in the pillows, and with the sheet drawn over her head, deaf to all comfort or words of sympathy. For who could comfort her when the appalling fact remained unchanged that her father was going to leave her, to go to the war, and she would be left alone?

In vain Fritz had stood by her bed and called to her.
He had brought her a box of the most delicious
sweetmeats, a farewell present from the confectioner;
for poor Madame Bellard, like all the rest of the French
residents in Edelsheim, had had to break up her home
since the war was declared, and prepare to leave Ger-
many at once; and now, as her shop was being closed,
the children of the neighbourhood were profiting by
her good-nature. To Violet she had sent a special
gift of great beauty—a box of frosted silver, and all
within were sweetmeats of various colours, pale pink
and green and white, which shone glitteringly, as if
they had been sprinkled over with diamond dust.

But no words of Fritz, nor descriptions of the treasure he held in his hand, could induce Violet to look
up. Her head was buried in her pillows, and no
sound but smothered sobbings reached his ears. Once
a little thin hand was stretched out for a moment
through the sheets, and grasped his gratefully, and
there was an effort to say something, but Fritz did
not understand it; and having left the sweetmeat-box
on the table beside her bed, he moved away dejectedly,
followed by Ella, who, in endeavouring to walk out
on her tip-toes, had nearly fallen down on her face in
the doorway.

Once in the afternoon Violet started up, and lifting herself painfully from the pillows, flung the clothes from off her face. She had heard a step on the stairs, and now she heard her father's voice calling to her. He was standing in the doorway as she looked up, and all the bright colour rushed to her pale face, and an exclamation of admiration and surprise burst quite unconsciously from her lips.

"Father, is it thou ? Oh, how splendid !"

And splendid he did look this afternoon in his new uniform—a giant in height, in breadth, in strength, with a fair open face, which could look stern enough at times, but now there was no sternness about it, only a searching eagerness to see if he might win one smile from his darling in the bed yonder.

John had to take his helmet off to enter at the doorway. And now, as he stood by his little girl's bed, turning himself round with an assumed pride for her admiration, he looked, as he was, one of the very flower of the German army, ready to die for his king and fatherland ; with a heart of steel to face the foe, and a heart of wax to be moulded by those tiny burning fingers in the bed, into whatever shape or form she chose.

"Has the king seen thee, father ?" she asked with a sob and a smile.

"No, my child."

"Ah, he will be delighted. Thou art the finest
soldier I ever saw."

"Thou thinkest so, my treasure?"

"Yes, yes; the best soldier in all the army"—she
stretched out her arms lovingly, yearningly—"and
the best, the very best, the dearest father in all the
world."

John put down his helmet on the bed; his sp
clattered, his sword clanked, as he stooped o͟v   n-
but she heard nothing—only the whisper in he   int
"Violet, my heart's treasure, how can I go aw   ls
leave thee?"   )   we

Later on in the evening, when he had gone.
make some final arrangements, and to buy some last
comforts for his little girl, and she had relapsed into
her former state of speechless grief, there came a tap
at the door of her room, and a voice, which seemed
to thrill through every fibre of her frame, cried
softly,—

"Is Violet awake? May Aunt Lizzie come in?"

Violet once more flung down the clothes and made
a violent effort to rise up quickly. Her cheeks flamed
to a carmine red, her eyes glowed in the twilight, and
there was something in their expression which made
her aunt pause on the threshold and place her hand
suddenly upon her heart.

" Poor little girlie ! all alone ?" she said, in the same
sweet, low voice. "Aunt Lizzie has come at a good
time to sit and comfort thee."

Violet had not seen her Aunt Lizzie for two long
years; but now, at this crisis of her young life, when her
heart was hungering for a face which she could never
see again, and her spirit was crying out for her lost
⋮⟨ her to comfort her, Aunt Lizzie had come in at the
sut℩. with the same gentle voice, the same sweet blue
fact ' nd waving golden hair, and had laid just such a
9⟨' ⟨k against her own. All Violet's reserve gave
theeϵ, ⟩nce, and she turned with a sudden movement
⟨powering relief, and flung her arms around Aunt
Lizzie's neck.

" Aunt Lizzie ! Aunt Lizzie ! dost thou know, hast
thou heard ?—my father— ;" here she turned her head
in upon her aunt's breast ; she could not finish the
sentence—only a storm of sobs completed it.

" Yes, yes ; I know it all. Thy father has to go
away to the war. It is terrible. I was thinking of
thee all the way in the train, and of all the other poor
little children in Edelsheim who must say ' Good-bye '
to-morrow to their fathers."

" But, Aunt Lizzie, Violet will be so lonely, so quite
alone."

" Yes ; thy father is so wonderfully good, and so

kind, thou wilt miss him more than most children : I know that well."

"There will be no one to sit with Violet all day, no one to kiss Violet at night, no one to hear Violet say her prayers, no one to talk about mother—only Kate, and Kate never knows what Violet says."

"Ah, well, Aunt Lizzie must think of some one to come and stay with Violet. Our little darling must not be left alone. We will talk to father this evening. And now Violet must dry her eyes. Aunt Lizzie has seen so many tears to-day that she feels quite sad ; and, besides, when father comes home we must not weep."

"Where did Aunt Lizzie see so many tears ?" asked Violet, still sobbing.

"Oh, so many!—such red eyes and blistered faces !—at the railway station. It was at first almost impossible for Aunt Lizzie to find a seat. Only the colonel interfered, and said they must make a place for her. So many wives with babies in their arms, sobbing and stretching out their hands ; and quite old women from the country, and little girls about thy size."

"Violet cannot go down to the station and see her father off to the war, can she, Aunt Lizzie ? "

"No, no; it would only make father sad, and it would tire thee."

"Were there any poor little hunchbacks at the station at Edelsheim?"

"What?" cried Aunt Lizzie, with almost a start of horror. "Sweetest treasure, thou must not say such things. Thou art our own sweet Violet—a little sick girlie that every one loves, and God most of all. Is it not so, my loved one?"

"Some hunchbacks have wings," said Violet, with a sudden gasp and a swift upward glance at her aunt's face. "God gives them wings."

"Yes, dearest child; and some day he will give thee wings too, and then Violet will fly away and be at rest: she will be so happy up there with mother; and she will have no more pain in her poor back, and she will never cry any more, nor have tears in her eyes."

"Yes," said Violet, with a sigh and a long, fluttering sob, "no more tears. The poor little hunchback in the fairy tale never cried once, not once, after God gave her wings. I read that in the book, underneath the picture, and I know it is true, although Fritz will not believe it, for I found the words in mother's Bible."

"Yes, yes, it is quite true," said Aunt Lizzie softly: "there will be no more sorrow nor trouble of any kind in heaven—nothing to make us cry—no more fighting, no more wars."

"No more soldiers, and having to say 'Good-bye,'"

added Violet sobbing. "Aunt Lizzie, Aunt Lizzie, Violet cannot say good-bye to father."

"Ah, darling, it is hard, but thou must try to say it;" and Aunt Lizzie pressed the little head close to her breast. "Father is a soldier, and Violet must seek to be a soldier too. Thou wilt be brave, sweetest child, for his sake, wilt thou not? Father's heart is breaking at having to say farewell to his little girl, and yet thou seest, dearest one, how he strives for thy sake to be cheerful."

"I know a text about soldiers, Aunt Lizzie," said Violet almost in a whisper.

"What is it, my little girlie?"

"'Fight the good fight;' but, Aunt Lizzie, Violet is too sick to fight, and her back aches so."

"Violet is one of Christ's own little soldiers, and when she is very tired she must just lay her head on his breast, and he will fight for her all her battles, whatever they may be."

"Yes; that is like mother's hymn that we used to say always at night, 'How sweet to rest on Jesus' breast.' And then when mother used to lie down beside Violet on the bed, and put her arms so closely around her, Violet used to say, 'How sweet to rest on mother's breast;' and there was no harm, was there, Aunt Lizzie?"

"None, none," replied the young mother with an effort to keep back her own tears. "Now lay thy head softly down on Aunt Lizzie's breast, and she will sing thee to sleep."

"Dost thou know what Kate said to Violet once?" asked the little girl, a smile spreading over all her face.

"No, my child; what was it?"

"She said Violet would soon sleep on mother's breast, and then Violet would have no more headaches. Is not that lovely, Aunt Lizzie?"

"Lovely," she answered almost in a whisper.

While they were talking thus, John came in. At first his face was somewhat white and stern. He seemed afraid to trust himself to glance towards the bed. When at last he did look across to the corner where Aunt Lizzie, who had taken off her hat and shawl, was sitting on the bed beside Violet, his face suddenly changed; a light, a look came into it, a sudden flush passed over his handsome face, and he stretched out his hand with a hasty movement and a quick outburst of thanks.

"Lizzie, thou best of sisters! so thou hast come. I scarcely dared to hope it. It has been too good of thee to leave thy home; and of Henry, too, to spare thee." He kissed her affectionately, and sat down on

the edge of the bed, where Violet lay, partially supported by her aunt's arm.

"Ah, God be thanked, my task is now com-
paratively light." He drew a long, deep breath, and
tried to smile a happy smile as he gazed into his
little girl's face and lifted one of her hands into his
own. "I have had such a busy afternoon," he continued, still searching into the large wistful eyes
opposite him for some ray of cheerfulness. "I have
finished Violet's carriage, and I have bought a lovely
cushion for it, and a rug to put over her feet; and
Fritz put Ella into it, and found it was so light he
could draw her up the steep hill from the church to
the fountain without drawing breath: so now Violet
can go out also every day and get some roses in her
cheeks.—Is that not so, my heart's angel?"

Violet nodded her head silently, and pressed her
father's hand, but no words came.

"And father is going to give Violet his canary to
take care of for him; and such a grand cage as he has
bought for him, all gold and silver, and with beautiful
green fountains. And Violet must feed him herself,
and see that he is never hungry or thirsty either.
Eh, my darling?"

"Yes, father."

"And here is a desk father has got for thee—a

real leather desk full of paper and envelopes and beautiful red sealing-wax ; and, look here, my treasure, a seal with ' Violet' on it. Is not that lovely ? "

" Beautiful," said Violet, her eyes dilating and her mouth expanding with a troubled smile.

" And somewhere in the desk Violet will find, if she searches well for it, a little box with silver in it, bright silver money to buy stamps with ; and when she wants more money in her box she must ask Madam Adler for it, and then she can always write letters to father and tell him all the news."

" Father will write to Violet ? "

" Of course, of course;—and the ink-bottle thou hast not seen yet, nor the pens and pencils," cried John with a sudden access of interest; for Violet's lips quivered ominously, and one large tear had already fallen with a splash upon the pink blotting-paper.

" And now we will shut up the desk, and Violet will get up on father's knee. We are all going to sit by the stove and have our supper. And father has a cake for thee, which Madame Bellard has baked on purpose for us. Wait till Aunt Lizzie sees it; it is all sugar on the top. It was good of Madame Bellard, in all her trouble, to think of us. Was it not, Violet ? "

" Yes, yes, too good," she said softly.

It did not take long to dress her. A couple of
shawls fastened loosely round her, and stockings
drawn up over her feet, were enough for the occasion;
and when the coffee was ready the cake was uncovered in all its glory. Such a splendid cake as it
was, all covered with creamy frosted white sugar; and
on the top were letters made of pink comfits, which
formed these words, "John and Violet;" and underneath, in smaller comfits of the same colour, was
added, "Auf wiedersehen" (To meet again).

Poor Violet! once her eyes fell on the pink-letters
it was with difficulty she could swallow any of the
cake. She put a small piece in her mouth, and
crumbled up the rest in her fingers, letting the
currants fall through them on the floor. She drank
her coffee eagerly, so as to swallow down the tiny
bits she had taken; and then John, watching her
closely, saw it was no use to offer her any more.

"We must give some of this grand cake to Kate,"
he said presently. "We cannot allow Aunt Lizzie to
eat it all. And Fritz, too, and Ella, they must each
have a slice." He took up the knife and began to
carve the cake with some recklessness.

Violet watched him intently as he cut a large piece
for Kate, then another for Fritz; and the knife was
already buried in the frosted silver for Ella's slice,

when she suddenly stretched out her hand and cried
out piteously,—

"No, dear father, not there. Ah, leave that piece
for me. Do not cut off those words; Violet loves
them."

John drew out the knife and laid it on the plate.
"Aunt Lizzie shall cut Ella a slice by-and-by," he
said softly; then drew his girl so close in to his side
that Violet could feel the loud beating of his heart.

After all, the supper proved but a sorry meal,
though Aunt Lizzie talked and laughed and told
anecdotes about her children at home, some of which
caught Violet's attention, and drew forth questions
and answers; but every now and then a deep unconscious sigh from John, or a smothered sob from
Violet, would show that their minds had wandered
far away from the little fair-haired children at Gützg-
berg.

At last he got up and laid her down upon her bed.
"I must say good-night now to my darling," he said
wearily as he stretched his arms up into the air.
"Father is very tired, and he must go down to the
barracks presently."

"Not to stay—not to sleep? Thou wilt not say
good-bye to-night?" cried Violet. "Dear father, not
to-night!" Her appeal broke into one long, pitiful wail.

" No, no ; not to-night.   Oh, darling child, if Violet
only knew how father's heart aches, she would not
cry so.   Try, sweetest darling, to be brave.   Father
will come back when he has reported himself to the
captain, and Aunt Lizzie will stay with thee while he
is away."

Violet ceased crying aloud, and lying back on her
pillows, resorted to her old device of drawing the bed-
clothes over her face.   John stooped down and kissed
the little hand that grasped them so tightly; then
saying a few words in a low voice to Aunt Lizzie, he
went out of the room.

When he returned about two hours later, Violet
was asleep.   Her aunt had sat by her bed and sung
to her, in a low, droning voice, little hymns and
nursery songs familiar to her ears in the old mother
days, until at last the sobbing ceased, the hand which
held the sheet gradually relaxed, and the child slept.

Poor John ! it was a relief to him to find all so
quiet in the room when he came up.   He had the
bird-cage in his hand, which he hung up on a peg in
the centre of the eight-sided alcove which formed the
window, and which jutted out some distance over the
street.

Then he drew a chair over into the alcove for
Lizzie, and they sat down in the gloaming to talk

over Violet and what was to be done to insure her happiness and comfort during the time he must be away at the war.

It was a long talk and a sad one, and to John, sitting there in the moonlit window, it seemed as if he were speaking in a dream to the poor little dead mother; for Aunt Lizzie listened with the same earnest sympathy, and when she replied it was in the same low tones. When she spoke, too, of the poor sick child lying now so quietly asleep on the bed in the corner, she used the very same expressions and endearing epithets of love, which came back to poor John's ears like whispers from the grave.

It was finally arranged between them that she was to remain with Violet for a few days after his departure, so as to allow the first burst of childish grief to pass over under her loving and watchful care. Then Aunt Lizzie had hoped that it might have been possible to have moved the poor little invalid to Gützberg, where she could have devoted herself to her charge, and she would have done so lovingly and faithfully. But John had already thought of this plan, and had consulted over it with the physician, a kind and clever man, who had known Violet from her birth; and he had decided against the plan, saying that any attempt to move the child from the room

where she had lived all her little life would be almost
certainly attended with fatal consequences. The
shock of a removal, and the tearing up of the frail
tendrils which held this little fading flower to life
would cause it suddenly to wither away. "And
besides," the doctor added kindly, "what should we
all do here in Edelsheim without our little Violet?
Why, you might almost as well take down the clock
out of the old church tower and tell us still to know
the time of day, as to take our Violet's face from the
window and tell us all to live pure and patient lives.
No, no, good man; leave us the child, and I for one
will watch over her."

So John had returned home with sudden tears in
his eyes, satisfied that the doctor was right. And Aunt
Lizzie afterwards confirmed him regretfully in the
same view; for she had said to Violet that afternoon,
when she was lying on the bed beside her, "How
would Violet like to leave Edelsheim for a little while,
just while father is away, and to return with Aunt
Lizzie to Gützberg? The little children at home
would scream with joy to have Violet amongst them,
and they would hold out their hands to welcome
her."

But the child had cried out almost in terror, "No,
no, no; do not take Violet to Gützberg. She must watch

for father at the window; she must wait for him till he comes home. He will not be long away. And besides, Aunt Lizzie, Violet could not leave her little mother. She is quite, quite close to Violet down there at the church; and sometimes Violet sends her flowers; and Fritz calls out quite loud, 'Mother, mother, Violet sends thee these flowers and her heart's love, and never, never forgets thee.' Fritz says it is all no use—she does not hear him calling out; but oh, Aunt Lizzie, Violet knows she does listen, for God hears all Violet's prayers, and father says my little mother is quite close to God."

After this outburst from the child's heart her aunt did not seek to urge her point. To tear asunder such strong links of love would indeed be death to Violet, and the little aching, loving heart, already half in heaven, must not be troubled further by any act of hers.

So now, all thoughts of Gützberg having been abandoned, it was arranged that a little maid called Evelina, who was at present in charge of Lizzie's children at Gützberg, should be engaged by John as nurse to Violet. She had been living in Lizzie's family for three years, and had a pretty bright face, a gentle manner, and up to this time had, under Lizzie's motherly direction, taken excellent care of the little ones. She was the only person Lizzie knew whom she could recommend from personal experience; and she undertook to impress on the girl's mind that she must, during John's absence, devote herself entirely to the sick child, and have no thought but for her comfort and happiness.

"One word more, Lizzie," said John, in a low, constrained voice, as he bent his head down on the back of Violet's chair, which stood empty in the moonlit window. "If—if, dearest Lizzie, it should please God that I should not return—what then? What is to become of my poor child?"

"God preserve us from such trouble," cried Lizzie, starting up suddenly, for there was a movement in the corner. "Hush! Violet will hear thee. Make thy mind happy. If I were to leave Gützberg and the children, and even Henry himself, I would come here and be a mother to her."

"It will not be for long," he said almost inaudibly as he lifted his helmet from the window seat and rose up. "The doctor told me so to-day. Thanks, a thousand thanks, good Lizzie. To-morrow at ten I shall be here to say good-bye. I shall have but a few minutes, that is all. We start at twelve for the front."

CHAPTER X.

AUNT LIZZIE slept beside Violet that night, with her arms tightly clasped around the little girl for whom the day was to break so bitterly. She found the soft breathing of the child, so peaceful in its restfulness, almost more difficult to listen to than the quick uneasy panting of the afternoon, for she knew well the anguish to which she must by-and-by awaken.

"So He giveth His beloved sleep," she murmured to herself as, in the summer dawn, she watched the little face so tranquilly turned towards her; and though occasionally there was a little fluttering sob, it was only a relic of yesterday's passionate weeping. Once when Violet smiled in her sleep and nestled more closely to her, Lizzie kissed her gently on the forehead. The child moved, smiled again, a broadening, happy smile, and said with a sigh of content, "On mother's breast."

Aunt Lizzie could not sleep. She watched the

bands of crimson rising slowly up behind the roofs opposite like streaks of blood. The cocks crew and screamed from yard, and garden, and barn. The fountain at the angle of the street dribbled and splashed monotonously. There was a child crying in an opposite house, bitterly, ceaselessly. The canary awoke, stretched its wings with the help of its thin yellow legs, took a drink at the green fountain, having eyed it first with suspicion, and then burst out into a loud joyous carol. Aunt Lizzie was afraid it would awake Violet; but she slept calmly on.

Then the sun itself rose up in all its splendour and shone gloriously over all. The red roofs blazed and glistened. The orange weather-cock on the chimney of Madame Bellard's house looked as if each separate painted feather on its wings were a tongue of fire, while the scarlet nasturtiums creeping up the red brick shaft trembled and glowed brilliantly.

Aunt Lizzie's mind, from the long night's watching, felt hot and confused. The rays of the sun which shone slantingly through the round old-fashioned panes of glass in the window threw stripes of prismatic colour on the floor and on the chest which held the dead mother's clothes and all the little relics of her homely happy life. If that bitter crying opposite would cease, Lizzie felt as if she could think con-

nectedly. If it were not for the fear of disturbing
Violet, she would have got up ere now and closed the
open pane in the window.

She tried to think of the little children at home at
Gutzberg, of their bright smiles, and hearts innocent
of care, but it was impossible. A drum in the distant
barrack had begun to throb, and her heart, leaping up
to a sudden agony, throbbed with it.

How many other hearts, too, were stirring at that
call! men buckling on their armour; and women, who
had not slept all night, starting up to fresh paroxysms
of grief and despair. It was vain to hope that all
the brave fellows going forth this day from their
homes would come back to them safe and unharmed.
Yet each one cried in their heart, " O God, let this
bitterness not come to me "—" Spare, good Lord, spare
my husband "—" Lord Jesus, have pity on my son "—
" Beloved, thou wilt return to me safe "—"Ah, dear one,
forget me not;" while the little ones smiled their
adieus, knowing not the dread future.

At six o'clock the whole town seemed astir. Men
were talking in the streets; spurs were clanking on
the pavement as soldiers hurried to and fro. Bugles
were calling, and the incessant rolling of drums
came now, not only from the distant barrack across
the river, but it seemed as if the whole air and

the blue sky itself were full of this dread pro
sound.

At seven o'clock, Lizzie, slipping her arm
from under Violet, got up and dressed herse ˌzie."
she came to the window, the first thinp
opposite was Ella. She was standing in
night-dress at the small top window in t where-
Her fair hair was partly tied back with ɾ ˌzzie this
night-cap, but stray locks hung ou
Her face was supported by her two ˈan ˌed hands,
and her elbows rested on the sill. It needed but one
glance at the child's face and eyes for Aunt Lizzie to
know who it was who had spent the night in such
ceaseless bitter weeping. Even now, though her
attention seemed temporarily attracted by the bustle
in the street, she saw the white frilled sleeve from
time to time passed quickly across the child's face.

In a few minutes Fritz appeared at the other little
window in the red roof opposite. He also was attired
in his night-dress; but he had a drum hung round his
neck by a piece of cord, on which, as he looked down
into the street, he began to beat with a prodigious
noise; and on his head was a newspaper cap, from
which streamed ribbons of scarlet, yellow, and blue.
When he was momentarily exhausted he flung open
the window, and stretched out his head excitedly.

almc. ˜ar, war, war!" he shouted. "Fritz will go to
comi? ?r. Fritz will beat the drum and kill the
and i and bang and hack and slash with all his
"He... every man is dead." A brass trumpet
stooped ?rally hung on a nail in the garret window,
"Let m? was often used by Fritz as a signal to
pinafore,?. et's attention, was now taken down and
for fathe? ?ently into the air; and then the drum
It will do? 'more vigorously than ever.

A few ?nose gathered beneath in the street
looked up on hearing the noise, and recognizing Fritz,
smiled somewhat sadly; but when Lizzie glanced
across again at the little window of Ella's room, the
child had vanished, and the drum having ceased
clattering for a moment, she could hear that the
crying in the room opposite had been resumed.

"How she does weep, poor little girl! and what a
noise the boy makes," said Lizzie, closing over the
casement. "He will certainly awaken our Violet."
She tried to attract Fritz's attention, to make him
desist, but finding it useless, she fastened the bolt and
turned back into the room.

To her surprise, on looking round, she found Violet
sitting up in her bed, her eyes wide open and her face
very pale.

"Aunt Lizzie?"

"Well, darling, hast thou been long awake?"

"A little while. When will father be here?"

"Very soon now."

"I do not want to say 'Good-bye,' Aunt Lizzie."

"No, darling, it is a hard word to speak."

"Will father say 'Good-bye' to Violet?"

"I suppose so. It is at least likely; but wherefore, darling child, dost thou ask Aunt Lizzie this question?"

"I do not want to say 'Good-bye,'" repeated Violet in the same sad voice. "It makes Violet cry to say 'Good-bye.'"

"Ah"—Aunt Lizzie paused with a little start as she suddenly recognized the cause of the child's distressful thoughts—"ah, I understand it. Violet would rather that there were no 'good-byes' said. Aunt Lizzie will tell father so, and he will understand what Violet wishes. Is not this what thou meanest, dearest child?"

Violet nodded her head. "Aunt Lizzie, what is Fritz shouting about over there at the window? and is not his father also going away to the war?"

"Yes, my child; and Fritz is screaming out that he will be a soldier too. He is a noisy lad, that Fritz."

"Violet wants to be a soldier too," said she in an

almost inaudible voice; "but father is so long in coming, and Violet's heart goes so quick, Aunt Lizzie, and it makes her sick."

"Here, let me smooth thy hair." Her aunt stooped quickly and kissed the little white face. "Let me bathe thy face and put on a nice clean pinafore, and then thou wilt look so bright and fresh for father. And now try and drink this cup of milk. It will do thee good."

She offered the cup to her, but the child shook her head. "I could not drink it. All the morning something is in Violet's throat, just here, and she cannot make it go down."

"Well, we will not mind the milk." Aunt Lizzie put the cup on the table, and brushed out her long fair hair and tied it up with her purple ribbon. She bathed her face with warm water from the sauce-pan on the stove, and the pinafore was already half over her head, when the door opened and John came in.

"Aunt Lizzie, is it father? Tell him, tell him quickly," cried Violet in a sudden tremor. "Violet cannot be a soldier unless thou tellest him first what I said to thee."

Lizzie turned from the bed, leaving the pinafore still over the child's face. John was already half-way across the room, and there was such a look of ques-

tioning anguish in his gaze as it met hers that she
could scarcely frame the words of poor Violet's re-
quest. She whispered, however, something in his ear,
which after a second's thought he readily understood;
and stepping over towards the bed, he waited until
Lizzie drew the pinafore down from his little girl's
face, gazing at her with the expression in his eyes of
one who waits with a speechless pain and dread to
look on the features of the dead.

But what was this! When the face was uncovered
there was a smile, an actual smile on her lips, and
one which grew with the mounting colour in her
cheeks as she stretched up her arms quickly and said
in a hurried whisper, " Father, Violet has been waiting
for thee."

" Yes, darling, I am somewhat late, but it was with
difficulty I could push my way up here through the
streets. I thought at one time I should hardly have
been able to force my way through them at all, and
that I should have been forced to say ' Good-bye ' from
the street."

" From the street ? " cried Aunt Lizzie and Violet
in one breath.

" Yes; the colonel has decided that we are to march
through the Market-place and then down by the fountain and along past these windows to the station."

"And I shall see thee again, father?"

"Yes, my darling."

"Aunt Lizzie will hold me in her arms, and I will look out at thee from the window."

"Yes, little treasure, yes."

"And Violet will watch thee coming up the street; and then she will see thee all the way along, along, until at last she will look, and look—and will see thee no more." The smile had spread wider and wider, and the eyes fixed on his face had dilated and darkened to their deepest purple; but now there came a sudden pause, and the lips trembled. It was evident the struggle could not last much longer. The little heart was brave, but the flesh was weak.

"Father, I have a secret."

"Yes, my own Violet; what is it?"

He stooped down, and Aunt Lizzie moved away.

"Dost thou see my face, father?"

"Yes, yes; the sweetest face in all the world."

"But dost thou see it, father?"

"Yes."

"Put thy arms round my neck, and I will tell thee Violet's secret."

He put his arms round his little daughter, and held her tightly to his breast while she placed her lips to his ear. "Violet is a soldier. The Lord Jesus can make even little sick girls brave. And, father, listen; look once more at Violet's face; look at her eyes." There was a pause, and then came the whisper, scarcely more than a fluttering breath— "Dost thou not see ?—no more tears."

He held her back for one moment and looked into her eyes. He kissed her passionately twice; then recognizing that this whisper was his darling's fare-well, he drew her to his heart with one long, silent pressure, and turned away quickly. One moment he gazed from the window, then stretching out his hand to Lizzie with averted face, he passed out into the street.

CHAPTER XI.

THE BUNCH OF VIOLETS.

FOR a long time after John left the room Lizzie did not look round at Violet. She could not trust herself to do so. Bitter tears were running quickly down her own cheeks, and she dreaded to see the face of the child, so she sat by the stove and covered her eyes with her hands, grieving, oh, so sorely, that there was yet another farewell to be gone through, and that Violet's small stock of strength and brave little spirit must be tried still further.

She was surprised, therefore, when about a quarter of an hour after John's departure Violet called to her in a low, quiet voice,—

"Aunt Lizzie, is the flower-shop far from here?"

"No, my darling; it is only just round the corner."

"I mean the stall where Fritz buys the flowers for mother. I forget the name."

"I do not know the name either," replied her aunt, rising and brushing the tears off her face; "but yesterday afternoon, when I was walking from the station, I noticed beautiful flowers for sale in a shop close to this house."

" Didst thou see any violets there ?"

" Yes, plenty of them."

There was a short pause, and then Violet said earnestly,—

" Aunt Lizzie, wilt thou go to the shop and buy me some violets ?   It is not far, thou saidst, and I have some money in my new desk."

" Of course I will go," said Aunt Lizzie, turning at once to look for her hat.   " Never mind the money, darling ; they will not cost much."

" But I should like to give the money.   And please, Aunt Lizzie, buy a large bunch, and very sweet. Sometimes Fritz buys violets that have no smell, and I do not care for them."

" All right; Aunt Lizzie will choose the very sweetest she can find.   And now here is the desk, and while Aunt Lizzie is tying on her hat thou canst take out the money."

Violet opened her new possession, and with trembling, eager fingers, removed the little secret receptacle which held her newly-acquired money and drew out several silver coins.

She placed them on the counterpane and waited for her aunt to turn round.

"Aunt Lizzie, wilt thou do one more thing for Violet ?"

"Certainly, anything. What is it, my little darling ?" for the child's face was covered with a crimson blush which darkened in its distress to almost a purple hue. "Darling, what is it ?"

"The cake, Aunt Lizzie, which father put by last night in the cupboard. May I have it ?"

"Certainly." Then, seeing her increased confusion, she added thoughtfully, "Aunt Lizzie is too glad that Violet should care to have the cake. It was made for thee, dearest, and madame would be so disappointed if thou didst not eat some of it."

Violet did not speak. She lifted her eyes nervously to her aunt's face, and moved her hands restlessly to and fro on the counterpane.

"I suppose I had better cut a slice for thee, the dish is so heavy ; and now I may give thee some milk, dearest. Thou hast had no breakfast."

"Please don't cut the cake, Aunt Lizzie."

"Well, here it is. I will put it on the table beside thee ; and here is the milk."

Violet nodded her head with that silent acquiescence which so often with her took the place of words, and Aunt Lizzie went down the stairs perplexed and wondering. When she reached the little side street she found the flower-stall literally besieged with women and children purchasing bouquets and bunches of flowers, to give to their dear ones ere they started for the war—beautiful blue forget-me-nots, moss roses, lilies of the valley. It seemed this morning as if the poorest child in the town had a penny to spare for this purpose.

Aunt Lizzie could scarcely force her way to the back of the stall, where a basket of sweet purple violets not yet unpacked had caught her eye.

"No, no," cried the woman excitedly as Lizzie put down her hand to select a bunch; "these cannot be touched until the others on the counter are sold."

"Oh, it is for a little sick child. I promised I would bring her home the sweetest in thy shop; and she will pay thee well, too, poor little girl."

"Who is the child?" asked the woman, curiously looking up at the young wife's pleading face, a something in the eyes and the voice stirring up old recollections. "Is it little Violet who has sent thee for them?"

"Yes, yes, the same."

"Take then what thou wilt, and from where thou wilt. There are even better bunches in the little tub under the table—real sweet violets from the king's garden; but they are not too good for her."

Lizzie knelt down and selected the finest bunch she could find in the tub——deep purple violets with the dew still on them and their stalks bound up with soft green moss.

" Thanks a thousand times; these are real beauties," she said gratefully. " How much do I owe thee for them ?" and she held out her hand, in the palm of which lay Violet's money.

" Nothing," said the woman quickly. " Go, take them to her ; she is welcome to them."

" But Violet wished to pay ; she will be grieved."

" Don't let her grieve, then. She has enough pain in her heart for this day, I warrant. If she says anything, tell her that I will call some day myself for my payment ; and that will be one look at her sweet little face. There, take a bunch of those blue forget-me-nots beside thee, and don't stop to thank me. My hands are too full this morning for such needless waste of time ;" and she turned away quickly to attend to her other customers.

Lizzie went back with her hands full of flowers and her eyes full of tears. How this little girl was beloved by all the town !——she a poor, sick, crippled child ; and yet she seemed to have cords of love binding her to almost every heart in the town. Aunt Lizzie smiled as she said to herself, " For of such is

the kingdom of heaven ;" and a vision full of comfort
passed before her eyes of the Lord Jesus standing with
outstretched arms waiting patiently to gather this
little suffering lamb into his arms.

When she reached the house she paused a moment
at the door, for she was anxious to give Violet time
to eat some of the breakfast which she had left beside
her, and, in the nervous state in which she had left
her, she felt sure the little girl would not be able to
do so if any one were beside her.   So, leaning against
the entrance door of the house with the flowers and
money in her hand, she stood a little aside from the
crowd, lost in a sorrowful reverie.

It was not until a figure had darkened the doorway for a full minute or so that she looked up and
perceived the policeman standing in front of her.

" How goes it with the little girl upstairs?" he said,
in a dry, matter-of-fact voice.

" Pretty well, thank you," she replied, wondering
at the interruption.

" Does she sleep? can she eat? is she heart-broken?"
He spoke abruptly, and Lizzie noticed with surprise
that his lip was trembling beneath his thick frizzled
mustache.

" She is making a brave fight," replied she warmly ;
" but the worst is to come."

"Yes, that is it," he said quickly. "Once he is gone there will be no keeping her. She will fade away, poor little flower, and be no more seen. Good-morning. It is well for her to-day that she has one kind heart to fly to."

He touched his hat with military punctilio as he departed, but his eyes, which looked straight before him out into the street, were full of tears.

"How does he know about her?" thought Aunt Lizzie wonderingly as she went slowly up the stairs; "and what a soft heart he must have beneath that hard and battered exterior."

When she opened the door of Violet's room she found the child sitting up in her bed with her face flushed and her eyes unnaturally bright. She had her desk open on the counterpane beside her, and immediately in front of her, resting on her knees, was the piece of cake which yesterday she had refused to allow her father to cut.

Her aunt went over to the bedside with her bunch of deep purple violets and the blue forget-me-nots and laid them on the coverlet. As she did so, Violet looked up and said, rather wearily,—

"Aunt Lizzie, canst thou help me?"

"Certainly; what is it?"

"It is so hard to print such a long word;" and she

pointed with a nervous hesitation to the pink letters on the cake.

Her aunt saw it all now—the little scrap of paper covered with almost illegible letters, and the shy action of the child to hide the effort from her eyes.

"Couldst not thou hold my hand on the pencil and show me how?" she asked almost piteously. "Violet prints so badly."

"Of course I can. Wait but one moment until I take off my hat and cloak, and we will do it beautifully together. It is not, after all, so badly done," she added comfortingly as she took up the paper and examined it. "I can read the 'Auf' quite plainly, and the other letters can be easily improved."

In a little time the words were printed quite distinctly—"Auf wiedersehen" (To meet again). Violet drew a deep breath as they were finished, and lay back on her pillows; but after a time she roused herself up again and said,—

"Still one thing more, Aunt Lizzie. Violet wants to print her own name on the paper, all by herself. She must do it quite by herself alone; but thou canst print it first, and then Violet can do it afterwards ever so like."

Aunt Lizzie saw at once what the child wanted, and so one letter at a time was drawn by her on a separate piece of paper, and Violet copied it painfully, until at last, with many shaky strokes and trembling uplines and places where there were no lines visible at all, the name " Violet " was printed in, crookedly enough, beneath the farewell words of love and hope.

" ' To meet again '—those are lovely words, Aunt Lizzie, are they not ?" and Violet smiled, for her task of love was finished.

Then with hands that trembled painfully she fastened the crumpled paper to the bunch of violets lying on the bed, and looked up at her aunt.

" I will not put these," she said simply, touching the blue flowers, which lay beside the other bunch on the counterpane. " Father will not forget his Violet ; for thou seest I am his little Violet—am I not, Aunt Lizzie ? and he would much rather have those. I know he would."

There was such questioning anxiety in her eyes that her aunt hastened to reassure her.

" The violets are far the best," she said with deci- sion. " The forget-me-nots are a present from the flower-woman to thyself."

" Oh, how kind—how lovely !" she said, almost in a whisper, as she lifted the blue flowers to cover the fast- rising blushes which the painful excitement of the moment kept ever driving to her cheeks.—" Aunt

Lizzie, what is that?" She started up with a bitter cry. "It is the drum, it is the drum, and Violet is not dressed."

It *was* the drum. Her aunt went over to the window and looked out. Far, far away, down at the foot of the hill close by the church, she could see soldiers marching out of the Market-place and defiling into the square in front of the large fountain.

"Aunt Lizzie, is it the drum? Violet knows it is the drum, and she is not dressed to see father go by."

The cry grew to a shriek. Lizzie's face was deathly pale as she turned round, but she said quietly,—

"Do not fret, thou dear angel. Aunt Lizzie will put on thy dressing-gown and hold thee in her arms at the window."

"Quick, quick!" screamed Violet, snatching up the bunch of violets; "they are coming quite close; I hear them."

"They are still a long way off," said her aunt reassuringly; "it will take them nearly ten minutes to reach to the top of the hill."

"But my father—he will watch for me, he will look up for me; he will think I am not there."

"Hush! quiet a moment, or I cannot lift thee in my arms. Oh, what a little tiny thing thou art! Now where are the violets?"

"Here, here," cried the child, stretching out her hand; "now open the window quick! Aunt Lizzie, there he is; I see him. My father! my dear father!"

The band was playing a familiar martial air, the drums thundered and shook the air, the trumpet-blasts seemed to cut all hearts in sunder; the old men and children in the windows screamed and shrieked, while the women in the streets, rushing along wildly beside the soldiers, uttered loud cries and bitter lamentations; and yet above all was heard one voice, one little child's voice, uplifted high in its misery.

"My father! my father! look up, look at thy Violet; she is here at the window.—Aunt Lizzie, hold me tight. I cannot see. The ground is moving. My father, where is he? I saw him a moment ago."

"He is just approaching; he is now beneath thee in the street, darling. Lean out; Aunt Lizzie will not let thee fall."

"Father, father! farewell, farewell! come back to Violet."

She flung the violets, as she spoke, far out into the quivering air. They fell first upon the heads of the surging crowd beneath, and then upon the ground. The men were marching on, John had passed by, and Aunt Lizzie groaned as she saw that in another moment they must be trampled under foot; but while Violet still cried aloud, " Farewell, farewell," some one in the crowd had pushed forward, stooped down hurriedly, and picked them up. It was the policeman ; and with a quick onward rush he had overtaken John in his march and thrust the flowers into his hand.

John gave one glance at the little paper, which had unrolled itself in its fall and displayed its farewell message to his aching eyes.

He turned his head, waved the violets high above his shining helmet, and looked lingeringly back at the face so deathly pale at the open window.

"He sees thee, my darling; he is waving his hand to thee," cried her aunt with choking tears.

"Farewell, farewell, farewell—'To meet again,'" cried Violet with failing voice. "Dear father—'To meet again'—to—;" but the black moving mass had passed out of sight, the helmets had ceased to glitter, and Violet's head sank on Aunt Lizzie's shoulder with a sob.

CHAPTER XII.

THE SILVER WATCH.

THE regiment had at length passed by, and the sound of the drums and trumpets had become almost inaudible, when Aunt Lizzie rose to lay her sobbing burden on the bed.

"So, my little loved one, we must rest now," she said softly; "and Aunt Lizzie will lie down beside Violet while she tries to sleep."

But at this moment a bell over her head rang with a somewhat sharp clang.

"What is that?" she said, pausing astonished with the child in her arms.

"Oh, it is nothing; only the basket-bell, Aunt Lizzie."

"The basket-bell? what is that, and where is it?"

"The bell is over Violet's chair, and the basket is in the street," replied the child wearily. "Lay me down, Aunt Lizzie, for Violet's head aches so."

Lizzie laid the child on the bed, and shook up the pillows. The bell rang again.

Aunt Lizzie crept over to the window quietly and looked about her curiously, till presently, catching sight of a red cord attached to Violet's chair, she imagined she had lit on the right object. She drew it up inch by inch, and by-and-by the little straw basket made its appearance at the window, and she lifted it in.

She hesitated a moment, then seeing Violet's eyes open she asked her softly,—

"Am I to open it, darling? or shall I give it to thee?"

"Do thou open it, Aunt Lizzie; Violet is too tired."

Her aunt drew out with some surprise a small package, most carefully fastened up and sealed. On the outside was printed in a clear strong hand,—"For little Violet, from a friend."

"This must be a present for thee, my child; something very precious it seems too."

"Oh, not now; put it away, Aunt Lizzie; Violet's head aches so."

"What! thou wilt not even look at it?" cried her aunt, whose own curiosity was now somewhat raised, and she carried the package over to the side of the bed; but Violet only pressed her head down into the pillows and waved the gift away with her hand.

"Aunt Lizzie, Aunt Lizzie, my head it aches so.

Come and sit beside Violet; for her father, her good, dear father, is gone away, so far away; and what can she do—what can she do—what can she do?" There were sobs, but as yet no tears.

"Thou canst pray to the good God to keep him safe and well," said her aunt softly, as she laid the packet on the table; "that will do thee good."

But while she stooped down and comforted the child with kisses and loving words, there was a knock at the door, and she cried softly,—

"Oh, who comes now? the child is tired and must sleep."

But it was the doctor who opened the door and walked in. He had promised John, the night before, to look after little Violet in the first access of her trouble; and as he walked towards the bed, she gave him a little smile of welcome.

He sat down beside her, drawing his chair quite close up, and took the little girl's hand in his, looking earnestly at her for a few minutes without speaking.

Violet blushed one of those painful blushes so common to her now, which flooded all the poor pale face with vivid carmine.

"What is this?" said the doctor, turning his eyes slowly away from her and looking at the sealed package on the table close to him; "what have we

here? A present for Violet, 'from a friend.'" He
took it up in his hand and examined it carefully.
"Thou hast not opened it yet, I perceive."

"No; some other day," she said softly.

"Why some other day? why not now?" and the
doctor held out the packet to her.

She stretched out her hand nervously; but it
trembled so, and the parcel was so weighty for its
size, that it fell from her grasp on the counterpane.

"There, there, that is enough; I will open it for
thee." The doctor took it up and broke the seal,
looking at it curiously as he did so. It had on it
a little bird flying out of a cage, with the simple
motto over it, " Free at last."

Inside the first paper was a layer of soft pink
cotton wool.

"It must be something very precious," said the
doctor, adjusting his glasses.

Violet rose a little on her elbow and looked also.

"Ho! I have a guess; but I can scarcely believe it
possible."

"What?" she asked in a low voice, scarcely conscious even that she spoke, and with her eyes riveted
on the parcel, from which the doctor was now slowly
removing the pink wool.

"Oh, wonderful! I have guessed rightly. It is what I thought; and this is a gift for thee, Violet."

"But what is it? I cannot see it." She rose now entirely from her pillows. "O Aunt Lizzie, see—it is a watch!"

"A watch!" cried her aunt excitedly, who had been standing all this time by the bedside with her eyes full of tears; "is it possible?"

"A watch for me!—how beautiful!" Violet held it in her hand, gazing at it with those deep purple-coloured eyes which spoke so often to those she loved, even when the mouth was silent.

"Let me look at it again; it is quite a beauty." The doctor took it in his hand. It was a silver watch with a double case—a case which opened with a spring to show the face. The back was all chased with the ordinary criss-cross lines, only in the centre there was a small round space with a name carved on it; and on the opposite side there was a space also, filled in with a wreath of blue forget-me-nots in enamel.

"Oh, how strange! I have certainly seen this watch before. Let me try if I could read the name." The doctor rose, and going over to the window adjusted his glasses with great accuracy. "It is just as I thought—'Margaret.' And who is the friend who has given our little Violet this beautiful present?"

"I do not know," she said, shaking her head; "it came in the basket."

"In the basket?" said the doctor; "and there was no name?"

"None," replied Aunt Lizzie. "I drew it up myself, and took out the parcel; that is quite certain."

"Then I must tell no tales," said the good old man smiling; "only Violet, I know, will take great care of the present;" and turning back he replaced the watch in her hand.

"Yes," said she softly; but her eyes were full of question.

"It belonged once to a little sick girl whom I knew well, and who is now an angel in heaven," he said in a low voice.

"A little sick girl," repeated Violet, gazing at him with eyes widening and darkening.

"Yes; she died early this spring, just when the flowers were beginning to shoot up and the larks to sing. She just stretched out her wings like the little bird on this seal, and flew straight up to heaven."

"Her wings!" cried Violet with a gasp; "was she—;" she paused again, colouring painfully.

"Was she what? what is it, my poor little girlie?" asked the doctor kindly.

"Was she a little hunchback like me?"

" A what ? what does the child say ? " cried the doctor in evident distress.—" Yes, she was like thee ; and I will tell thee why : Because she was one of the sweetest little maidens in the world ;" and with a sudden tenderness he stroked back Violet's hair and kissed her on the forehead. " She was one of the Lord Jesus' own little lambs ; and when she was very tired and very sad she told him all her trouble, and he loved her and comforted her."

" Yes," said Violet with a little trembling sigh, and enormous tears rising up and clouding her eyes.

" And now," he said, sitting down by the bedside and taking the child's hand, " we must feel Violet's pulse with this new watch and make it useful."

What a burning little hand it was, and how the poor heart was beating ! There was no need to look at the minute hand, for the thread of life leaped on at a countless speed, and the doctor closed the cover with a snap.

" Violet is a good girl ; she will take the medicine I shall send her presently."

She nodded her head, and as she did so the tears fell out of her eyes upon the linen sheet. She looked up swiftly, deprecatingly at her aunt.

" She has been such a good girl all the morning," said Aunt Lizzie ; " she has been so brave, our Violet.

She would not shed a tear to fret her father or make his heart ache. I think now we may let her cry a little; is it not so, sir?"

"Certainly; it will do her good to cry." The doctor's voice was husky, and he dropped his glasses quickly, so that they clinked against the buttons of his coat. "I shall send her up now at once a little draught, very small, and without a bad taste; let her take it the moment it comes; and try and keep the room and the house quiet. We must get her over this day and night somehow," he added as he reached the door. "Of all the patients I shall have to see this afternoon there is not one for whom my heart aches as it does for the little maiden yonder. The sorrows of this world will not trouble her long. Good-evening;" and going down the stairs, the doctor blew his nose sonorously and went out into the street.

The thoroughfare was almost deserted now. The women had gone back into their houses to weep and pray; and the men, what able-bodied men there were left, had resumed their daily toil. It seemed as if a great fire had died out of the heart of the town and left nothing but ashes behind it. Only the clank of the policeman's sword could be heard resounding through the empty street, clinking slowly against the stones of the pavement.

"Good - evening," said the doctor as they met presently face to face; "how goes it with thee, William ? I suppose thy son is off with all the rest of the lads this morning."

"Yes, doctor."

"It has been a hard day for thee, no doubt."

"Yes, hard enough ; though, the good God pardon me, I nearly lost sight of the poor lad, watching the girl up at the window yonder throwing the violets to her father. It was enough to make one's heart-strings crack."

"She reminds thee of thy little Margaret, no doubt," said the doctor kindly. "I have seen the likeness; and I have also seen the joy which thy kind heart has procured for her this afternoon, at perhaps the most critical moment of her life."

"God be praised !" said the policeman earnestly. "Can she, will she live, do you think, until he returns ? "

"Heaven only knows," replied the doctor as he nodded his farewell. "It is well for those good friends who are already at rest."

CHAPTER XIII.

NOISY FRIENDS.

THE next morning Fritz and Ella came over quite early, before Violet was up, to see her. Her head ached still, and Aunt Lizzie had advised her to stay in bed until after her dinner. All night she had lain with the silver watch clasped in her hand, and all the morning too she had held it tightly pressed in towards her. "It had belonged once to a little girl who was now in heaven;" that had been the burden of her thoughts ever since she had heard its history. "This little sick child had stretched out her wings and flown straight up to God." The doctor had said so; and she remembered a day, long ago, when she had heard her father say to her mother that the doctor was the best and kindest man in all Edelsheim. And then poor Violet, burying her head deep down in the pillows, had said, in a low voice of entreaty, "O good Lord Jesus, give Violet wings, too, and take her soon to heaven."

Fritz was, for him, quite nervous when he first entered the room, and Ella kept as much in his shadow as possible. Every one in the house and in the street had been talking about Violet, and her great trouble since the departure of the regiment; and Fritz had come to look upon his little friend as a kind of curiosity, to be approached with an unusual degree of compassion and gentleness.

But the ruse of the old policeman, to distract her thoughts for a time, had succeeded almost beyond his hopes. She was quite like herself this morning, and stretched out her hand at once to her playfellows affectionately, and said with some excitement,—

"Fritz, look at my watch."

"Thy watch! Who gave it thee?"

"I do not know," she said, with a slow, sweet smile; "it came in the basket. It has got forget-me-nots on one side, and Margaret on the other; and the little girl it belonged to is in heaven."

"How dost thou know?"

"The doctor said so. She was very very sick, and when the flowers and the larks came, God gave her wings, and she flew right up there."

"Where?" asked Fritz.

"There; far away, over the roofs and over the

steeple, high, high ; ever so high up, up, till at last she
was with God."

"And who was she ? what was her name ?" questioned Fritz.

"I do not know," said Violet, shaking her head.
"But, Fritz, I was wondering. I was thinking all
last night that perhaps it was the same little sick girl
who had the book. Thou rememberest, dost thou not ?
It came in the basket too."

"What book ?"

"About the little hunchback," said Violet in a
whisper.

"Oh!" cried Fritz, with quite a visible start; "yes;
of course I remember the fairy-tale book. We thought
at first it was the girl with the oranges; but she cannot be in heaven, because I saw her to-day."

"No, not a bit of that girl is in heaven," cried
Ella joyously. "Fritz and I saw her to-day. Fritz
climbed up the steps, and gave her hair a chuck; and
she jumped round so fast that she fell over, and bumped
down every step—bump, bump, bump—and all the
oranges galloped after her. When she got to the
bottom," screamed Ella, "she was sitting in the middle
of her own basket, and her heels up in the air—so;"
and Ella plumped down on her back on the floor, and
elevated two of the stoutest legs imaginable.

"She bellowed after us that she would call the police," cried Fritz, continuing the story with much zest; "but I screamed back to her that the police would put her in prison for sticking pins in her oranges and sucking them, as I have seen her do hundreds of times. Then she flew into a worse rage, and said that she would run home and tell her father. So Ella and I laughed, for she would have a long way to run to tell her father—would she not, Violet?"

"Yes," she said quickly; but the smile which had risen at the children's story suddenly died out from her lips.

Fritz said, "Perhaps she would have to run all the way to Paris; and it would be nicer to pick up oranges out of the gutter than cannon balls, and be bursted all to pieces by powder."

Aunt Lizzie cried "Hush!" and rose from her chair by the stove; but the children did not hear her, and went on excitedly,—

"And do you know, there has been fighting already, and lots of people killed; but not in our regiment," added Fritz hastily, for he was alarmed at the sudden agony that came into Violet's face.

"I saw the picture," cried Ella at the tip-top of her voice. "I saw it in the shop window—a man climbing up a great steep rock with no head on him at all.

It had just been banged off his body by a gun.   And
another man on his face, with only one leg.   And
dost thou know what Fritz said ?   If he had been
there the French people would never have got into
that town—not they, old blockheads as they are."

"What town ?" asked Violet, almost in a whisper.

"Saarbrück, near the Rhine.   But it was all a shabby
trick of the French ; so all the people say.   And we
will make them pay for it by-and-by ; see if we won't.
We will hunt them out of it again with cannons, and
powders, and drums."

"Yes, with powders and drums !" shouted Ella.—
"And dost thou know, Violet, Fritz wanted to go to the
war with father, and beat a big drum all day with an
apron on him ; and he screamed so, father said 'Perhaps.'   And all night Ella cried and cried, and never
stopped ; and in the morning father got out of his bed
and kissed Ella, and said Fritz must stay at home and
take care of me.   And Fritz was in such a rage he
tore Ella's night-cap in two, and flung it in the bread-
oven."

"Come, now, we have had enough noise for one
afternoon," said Aunt Lizzie quietly.   "Suppose we all
sit round the stove and let Violet rest ; her head has
ached all the morning, and she looks very tired."

"Oh no, Aunt Lizzie ; let them stay," said Violet ;

and she stretched out her hands to the children. "I have not seen Fritz for so many days, nor Ella either."

"Mother would not let us come," said Fritz bluntly. "She said thou wouldst be busy saying good-bye to thy father and crying, and it would be no use bothering."

"Yes, very busy crying," said Ella plaintively.

"And I am going to begin now and say my prayers," observed Fritz, whose eyes had suddenly rested on Violet's Bible lying on the table beside her bed. "Mother says Ella and I ought to pray every morning and every night for father to come home safe; and so I am going to begin to-night."

"And didst thou not always say thy prayers every morning and every night?" asked Aunt Lizzie in some surprise.

"Oh yes, I always say them," observed Fritz; "but I don't think about them; at least not much."

"He does not think about them one scrap," said Ella cheerfully; "he stares at the wall, and goes sound asleep; and sometimes he looks round at me, and begins to laugh; and sometimes he rattles his heels on the ground until mother comes up and smacks him."

Aunt Lizzie shook her head at this history; and Violet said in a very low voice,—

"O Fritz, is not Ella joking?"

"No," replied Fritz truthfully. "I don't much care for saying prayers. I like to ask God for things which I think he will give me, but it tires me to say the same thing so often. At least one month I used to pray every day for a lovely gray pony that was in the field, and I never got it. And, besides, every morning when I woke I used always to say to God, 'Good Lord God, make little Violet well;' and yet thou art still sick, and weaker and weaker. And then," continued Fritz, bending close down beside her, and speaking in a whisper, "once I prayed in the day, too, when I read that book about the little hunchback girl. I went straight home and asked God to give thee wings too; and yet thou hast never got them."

"Yes," said Ella in a very grave tone, having overheard the whisper, "he went straight home and locked the door, and would not let Ella in; and Ella banged and banged, and it was all no use. And then she put her eye to the keyhole, and Fritz was saying his prayers at the kitchen table; and Ella heard him say, 'Please, good Lord Jesus, put wings on Violet's hump, like the little girl in the story. Amen.'"

"Hush! we have had quite enough talking for one day," cried Aunt Lizzie again hurriedly, her face flushing crimson, as she gazed in anguish at the little sick girl in the bed. "Away with thee, Ella! away with thee too, Fritz! I cannot have my little girl tired."

But Violet flung her arms round Fritz's neck affectionately, and cried out gratefully, "Thou dear, good Fritz!" Then putting her lips to his ear, she said in a low whisper, "The Lord Jesus does always hear when Fritz prays, and he will give me wings, and he will do all that Fritz asks him."

CHAPTER XIV.

THE next day, about four o'clock in the afternoon,
Evelina arrived from Gützberg.   Violet had been told
that she was coming, and that she was to be her own
little maid and companion until her father returned to
Edelsheim from the war.   Aunt Lizzie, too, had promised that she would often come over and see her, and
Fritz and Ella would meantime be her daily com-
panions; and Madam Adler, too, had promised John
that she would be constantly on the watch, coming to
see that the child was well and happy.

"It will not be for *very* long, will it?" she had
said to her Aunt Lizzie, as she was being dressed that
morning for the first time since the departure of the
regiment.

"What will not be for long?"

"Until father comes home," replied Violet smiling.
" I heard him tell thee so that night when the moon
was shining through the window.   Did not he, Aunt

Lizzie?" The child's eyes deepened with prophetic joy as she gazed full into her aunt's face, waiting for a reply. It did not come at once, and she added with an ever-increasing smile, "And when the war is over I shall see him again, ever so soon. He will cry out, 'Where is my own little Violet?' and look up; and I will stretch out my arms—so—Aunt Lizzie; and then all the fighting will be over, and we shall never have to say good-bye any more."

Aunt Lizzie was drawing on Violet's stocking, and she bent her head very low to see that the seam was straight at the ankle. When she looked up again, the smile was still on Violet's lips, but her eyes were looking far away up into the blue sky, high, high up above the roofs and the steeple, to where the little sick girl, whose watch was beating so close to her heart now, had gone up to be with God.

When Evelina arrived, there was quite a little company gathered together to meet her—Aunt Lizzie, and Violet, and Fritz, and Ella, and Madam Adler, who had baked a special loaf for the supper, and who had also a curiosity to see the new girl, and form her own opinion as to her capabilities.

"What a huge box she has!" cried Fritz, who, full of interest, was kneeling on the cushioned window-sill, and could thus overlook the whole street. "And

another box, too, stuck up beside the driver; and
here she is herself, and two more boxes in her hand."

"Yes, two little, tiny baby boxes," shouted Ella,
whose rosy face was spread out against the window-
pane, "and two very black hands."

"Those are not her hands; those are her gloves,
little donkey," cried Fritz contemptuously. "I saw
her face; and she is ever so pretty.—She is indeed,
Violet, ever, ever so pretty."

Violet nodded her head in her grave, peculiar way.
It was a moment of intense excitement to her the
advent of this new girl, the friend who was to be
always with her until her father's return; but no one
could hear the throbbing of the little girl's heart.
And though her eyes darkened and the pupils grew
wider and wider, no one knew the tumult going on
within her breast.

As a rule, she took no interest in strangers. Like
all invalids, she shrank from the entrance of those
with whom she was not intimate; and those who
knew and loved her pitied her distress when the crimson blushes, rushing in waves over her pale face,
showed the nervous tremor of her heart.

But to form a really new friendship was a thing
almost impossible to her. She loved those whom she
had known all her life, with a tenacity far beyond

the usual love of children. She clung to them as all sick people cling to those who daily watch and tend them; and though Aunt Lizzie had sought in every way to inspire her with a feeling of confidence and interest in Evelina, she shrank from the thought of their first meeting. And now, as she heard the ascending footsteps, a sudden rush of unreasonable distrust and premature dislike seemed to fill her heart, and she turned her face quickly away towards the window, and held fast hold of Fritz's hand, who was standing with gaping mouth and eyes riveted on the doorway.

There was a little flutter in the room. Aunt Lizzie rose and moved towards the door; Madam Adler, too, went forward; Ella drew back a step or two from the stove; and Violet, still looking with straining eyes at the houses opposite, heard, as the door opened, a sweet voice saying, in reply to some question of her aunt's,—

"Yes, thank you very much; I have had a very good journey. It was almost stiflingly hot in the train, but the air is cooler now."

"And the children?" asked Aunt Lizzie.

"Oh, the little angels, they are as well as possible. They cried, of course, when I took leave of them; but the master is taking them out this afternoon for a

walk in the gardens; and the little one is quite happy.
—Ah, is that the little sick girl yonder?"

Violet turned her head quickly round and looked
up. ·

"Oh, how white she is!"

Aunt Lizzie hurried forward and stood beside
Violet's chair.

"Here, sweet one," she said, kissing her on the
forehead, "this is Evelina of whom we have talked
so much. Thou and she will be great friends by-and-
by. She has come all the way from Gützberg to take
care of thee; is it not so, my treasure?"

Violet nodded her head and smiled nervously, then
stretched out her hand to take Evelina's, but there
was no enthusiasm in the movement.

"Ah, the poor child, she is nervous, she is shy, but
we shall soon be the best of friends," cried Evelina
pleasantly; "one cannot expect the little one to take
to me all at once.—And who is this lad who looks as
if he would eat me with his eyes, eh?"

"I am Violet's own friend," replied Fritz, colouring
purple, but placing his hand firmly on the back of
Violet's chair.

"Ah, it is very pleasant for her to have such a
good friend," observed Evelina, laughing and throwing
back her head so that the little gold bells on her ears

tinkled;—" but by-and-by you must be my friend too ;
is it not so, eh ?"

" Perhaps," said Fritz shortly, while poor Violet
looked down at her pinafore and blushed because
Fritz was somewhat uncivil in his reply.

" And who is this little cherub with the red cheeks ?
is she also a friend ?" asked Evelina, as she sat down
on the cushioned window-seat and tried to lift Ella
on her knee ; but the child wriggled somewhat roughly
away from her, and a shower of wooden animals—
ducks, pigs, and camels—which had been arrayed
along the ledge overhead tumbled down in confusion
over Evelina's hat, shoulders, and lap.

This created a general laugh, in which even Violet
joined, and the first stiffness of the introduction was
in this manner happily got over.

Evelina had a very pretty and pleasant face. There
was certainly nothing to frighten one in it. Her
hair, which seemed one mass of frizzly, golden threads,
was brushed back from her face and pinned at the
sides with somewhat large gold pins ; she had eyes
that seemed ever sparkling and smiling, rosy lips, and
cheeks with dimples in them.

When she took off her hat and put on a very
dainty white cap with crimped frillings of lace, and a
snowy linen apron also edged with carefully-goffered

frills, she looked so fair and sweet and happy, that Violet's eyes became riveted upon her, and she followed all her movements with an unconscious interest.

At last the moment came for Madam Adler to say good-bye, and Fritz and Ella as usual took a loving farewell of their little play-fellow.

As Fritz flung his arms round Violet's neck, he said in a whisper,—

" She is very pretty this Evelina, but—"

" What," cried Violet, a sudden distress coming into her eyes; " what is it, Fritz ?"

" Nothing—I am not sure—I do not know; some other day I will tell thee;" and before she could drag his meaning from him he had marched across the room with head erect, and so he preceded his mother down the stairs.

CHAPTER XV.

WEIGHED IN THE BALANCES.

THAT "but" of Fritz's rested all the evening somewhat heavily on Violet's heart, otherwise there was something about Evelina that would perforce have fascinated the child. It was a face that seemed to grow prettier each time she looked at it; and her voice was so sweet, especially when she sang little snatches of song, which she did apparently unconsciously, as she went about the room setting everything in apple-pie order, and dusting the ornaments and furniture with an easy grace, as if all she did were a pleasure to her.

In the evening, after Violet had been put to bed, Aunt Lizzie went out to get some letters, and Evelina and her charge were left alone. The moment the door closed on her protectress, the nervous look came back to Violet's eyes, and she gazed with a distressed intentness at the shining brass balls at the foot of her bed.

Evelina, however, appeared quite unconscious of

any difference in her manner. She added wood to the stove, polished the brass kettle, chirruped to the canary, and then seating herself at the window, she took out her knitting, and with swiftly-flying fingers went on with a stocking which she was making for one of the little boys at Gützberg.

This she told Violet presently with much laughter, describing how the little tease Henry had pulled all the needles out of her work just at the most critical part, to make sticks for his soldiers' flags, and how she had had to go back and knit half the leg over again; and all the time that she laughed and told her story she was knitting away without once looking at her work, but straight out of the window at the houses and shops opposite.

Once when she looked up hastily, she became aware of two faces placed against the high-up window of a house almost exactly opposite, and she saw that four eager eyes were following all her movements with an intense interest.

In the fair, round, smiling face, with its great blue eyes, and its golden curls all tucked away inside a plain white linen nightcap, Evelina did not at first recognize Ella; but a glance at the burning eyes of the little boy who stood beside her, and who seemed to watch her own actions with an almost jealous anxiety, was sufficient to make her recognize the lad who had stood by Violet's chair that afternoon, and had replied so shortly to her question " that he was Violet's own friend."

" Ah, that is where he lives, thy little friend. How he does stare ! "

Evelina put down her knitting for a minute, and nodding across to Fritz, drew out her pocket-hand-kerchief and waved it through the open pane beside her.

Fritz bowed in reply rather stiffly. Ella pranced about in some excitement for a moment, but noticing that Fritz's expression was somewhat gloomy, she became grave also, and in a few minutes they both disappeared from the window.

Then, almost without being aware of it, Violet and Evelina fell into quite a natural talk. Evelina had so many questions to ask about Ella and Fritz, and their parents, and the people who lived on either side of them, and how they all were, and what occupations they had ; so that when Aunt Lizzie returned from her walk she was quite delighted to hear, as she placed her hand on the door, a quiet little laugh from Violet, as she exclaimed in evident amusement—
" Indeed he is not; he is a grand old fellow, and I love him."

" Old !" replied Evelina; " why, I should not call him old, and he is very handsome. I can see him now quite plainly, for he is looking up at me this moment."

. Evelina had risen, and was gazing out through the casement as Aunt Lizzie entered, so she did not hear her mistress's step until she was quite close beside her.

" Of whom art thou speaking, darling ?" asked Aunt Lizzie, glad to notice the smile which was still lingering on Violet's face.

" Of the old policeman. Evelina asked me if he was a very cruel man, and he is so good, Aunt Lizzie; he sometimes kisses his hand to me; and dost not thou remember it was he who picked up my violets and gave them to—to father;" there was a sudden break in the child's voice, and the smile died suddenly away.

" Ah yes, he is a good old fellow," replied her aunt quickly; " he spoke to me the other day and asked me all about thee."

" About me, Aunt Lizzie ?"

" Yes, darling, about thee. Violet has many friends in the town of whom she knows little, or perhaps nothing; but they know her—they look up at her as they go past the window, and they love her."

" They love me ?" Violet smiled again, an inquiring, happy smile, and her little white face mantled with modest blushes. "So many friends," she said softly; then added almost in a whisper, "and also, Aunt Lizzie, the Lord Jesus; he is my friend too, is he not?"

"He is indeed thy best friend; so good a friend, that no matter who else goes away and leaves little Violet, he is always beside her; and when she is very tired, and her back aches, and her heart is sad, then she has only to think how close he is beside her, and rest her little tired head just so against his breast." And as Aunt Lizzie spoke she drew Violet close beside her, and covered her upturned face with loving kisses.

Evelina was seated again in the window as Aunt Lizzie turned round from the bed. Her fingers were flying swiftly, the steel needles clattered and chinked, but there was a moisture in her usually bright eyes, which her mistress understood and was glad to see.

Two days afterwards Aunt Lizzie returned to Gützberg, leaving Evelina in sole charge of Violet. She had almost grown accustomed to her now. At first it was a sore trial to her that Evelina slept in the room which used to be her mother's. When the door of it opened and shut, her heart gave sudden leaps and starts, which made her sick and wretched. When she saw Evelina's hat hanging on the same nail where her mother's used to be, she turned her eyes away quickly; but even to this she soon grew accustomed, and said to herself, with a long, wishful sigh, "When father comes back all will be like home again."

Fritz, too, became much more friendly with Evelina as the days wore on. She had quite a fund of fairy tales and children's stories, which she used to tell them in the evenings. It was after supper was finished that they used to gather round her in the window; and Violet's eyes grew and darkened and deepened in the summer twilight as she listened, inthralled, to the stories of forest gnomes and elves that hid themselves beneath the fragrant ferns and mosses of the woods.

Evelina could sing, too. She had the sweetest voice imaginable, and she knew heaps of ballads; and when the song was an exciting one, she would act it with quick gestures and flashing eyes; or when it was sad, real tears sprung to them with an almost unnatural swiftness.

Violet listened and pondered and watched every movement of the face before her; and yet, with an unconscious distrust, still kept the whole freedom of her loving heart uplifted in the balance.

"Fritz," she said one evening suddenly, as he and

she sat alone in the deep window-seat, " Fritz, tell me this one thing: dost thou love Evelina?"

" I like her," replied Fritz quickly.

" I like her too, she is ever so kind to me, and she never says a cross word, like old Kate; but I like Kate better."

" I know," cried Fritz, who was busy peeling a stick and throwing the shavings on the ground, " she looks in the glass so often, and she is always twisting up little curls on her forehead. I can see her from the window opposite. And once she was smiling and bowing at herself in the glass, and she suddenly looked up and saw me; and she was such a little fool, she ran away with her face covered up with her hands and threw herself down on the bed. Still she is not too nasty," added Fritz comfortingly, " and I like her. She tells grand stories, and she is awfully good-natured."

Violet listened almost awe-struck. Fritz was certainly wonderful at guessing and seeing things; he knew much better all about Evelina than she did, and he was able to explain things so easily.

" She often says ' Yes' when she is not listening to one word any of us says; and when she leans out of the window and sings, she pretends she does not see the people in the street stopping to hear: she pre-

tends lots of things; that I see well enough," cried
Fritz, waving the newly-peeled white stick triumphantly over his head, and bringing it down on the
cushion with a bang. "Still I like her, and Ella
thinks her simply an angel."

Violet grew more reassured; and when Evelina returned smiling and pretty, and with a lovely fresh
cake full of currants in her hand for Violet, the room
seemed quite bright again; and Ella coming across
the street, and up the stairs with great bounds, was
kept for the evening meal, and sat on Evelina's knee
all the afternoon happier than any queen.

CHAPTER XVI.

FATHER'S LETTER.

So the long days deepened, and the sun grew hot and strong over the town of Edelsheim. In the middle of the day the streets were almost deserted, except by those who, under cover of huge, mushroom-shaped umbrellas, ventured out to make their purchases. Even the roofs opposite had been almost deserted by the birds, which only twittered in the early morning; and the pigeons pattered up and down in the shadow of the eaves, or sat huddled together on the chain which hung across the street opposite Violet's window, for at mid-day their pink feet would have been scorched on the hot tiles of the houses opposite, where they generally congregated.

Violet's canary seldom sang now. In the evening sometimes it trilled out a delicious song, with its head bent on one side, as if it were looking out through the opening in the roofs opposite to the hill, with its crown of trees and the blue sky over it so fresh and free; but in the morning it never sang. Evelina would not allow it to sing; its chattering and loud rejoicing as the sun arose had disturbed her sleep, and rising up early one morning, she had opened the door of her room suddenly, and with smothered, angry words, had rushed in and thrown a black shawl over the cage, which she had carried with her in her hand from the inner room. Violet, who was awake, and listening to her favourite's song with silent pleasure, protested loudly, but it was all of no use; Evelina was really angry, and she said sharply that if Violet chose to make a fuss about it she would remove the cage from the room altogether.

Violet's heart beat and her eyes flamed, and she cried hotly after Evelina's retreating figure.

"Father will soon come home, and then—"

"Yes; and then thou mayest do as thou choosest, no doubt, and eat the little beast, head and tail, if it pleases thee; but it shall not keep me awake, that is all." Evelina closed the door sharply after her, and flung herself back into bed, angry with Violet and angry with herself.

Both their voices had been raised, and the windows of the room lay wide open to catch even a passing breath of the cool morning air.

And as Evelina had hurried past the window of

her room she had caught a glimpse of the old policeman standing on the pavement opposite, and looking
up anxiously with strained inquiring gaze at the
projecting casement of Violet's room. He must have
heard her anguished cry of protestation, " Father will
come home soon, and then—" But her own voice,
she hoped, had not been raised so loud. " The little
spoiled thing! she thinks she must not be crossed in
anything," she said pettishly to herself; and so turning
on her pillow fell fast asleep.

The same morning brought a letter from Violet's
father, and her trouble about the canary bird was
soon forgotten. It was such a long letter. Her eyes
deepened and her cheeks flushed. She begged of
Evelina to go across the street and ask Madam
Adler to come over and read it out to her. Evelina
took the message somewhat unwillingly, saying that
she could read it for her with pleasure. But Violet
shook her head and replied nervously, " Madam
Adler knows father, and she will understand."

" I suppose," replied Evelina with a short laugh,
" any one who does not know thy father must be a
blockhead, eh ?" and running lightly down the stairs
and across the street, she came suddenly face to face
in the Adlers' doorway with the policeman.

Evelina blushed a deep conscious blush and tried

(789)   11

to hurry past; but laying his hand a moment on her
arm he said gravely, while he pointed across at the
window opposite,—

"How is the little maiden up yonder?"

"Oh, she is like a mad thing this morning. She has
got a letter from her father, and I have just flown
across to call Madam Adler to read it to her."

"So; that is good," he replied, still looking fixedly
at Evelina's blushing face, and seeking to fix the eyes
which looked every way except at him.

"Let me pass, if you please," she said nervously;
"the child will be impatient if I delay."

"You are very kind to our Violet?" he said, moving
a little aside.   "She is happy?"

"Oh yes, happy enough; that is to say when she
gets everything she wants. She is a trifle peevish
sometimes, and hard to manage. But we are great
friends."

"I fancied I had heard her crying this morning
very early; was it not so?"

"Pah!" cried Evelina with a toss of her head,
"one must not stand in the street and count every
cry a sick child gives. The canary bird chattered so
that she could not sleep, nor I either, so I threw a
shawl over its head, and there was an end of the
matter."

"So," said the policeman again, only this time more gravely, and allowed Evelina to go past him up the stairs.

Madam Adler did not lose a moment in hastening to come at Violet's call. She too had had a letter from her husband, and had only just read the first line; but she thrust it into her pocket and hurried across the street. Little Violet's trembling heart must first be quieted, and then when she was satisfied Madam Adler would return and read her own letter in the quiet of her room with many thanks to the good God who had spared her husband so far.

She drew her chair beside the bed, and having kissed the little white face with its ardent, loving eyes, she took the letter from Violet's hand and read it out to her slowly. It was just such a letter as she had expected it would be—overflowing with love, and with almost no allusion to the war or its horrors, but giving accounts of their camp-life,—the bivouacs under the trees, the fires lighted on the grass, and the large camp-kettles swung upon poles over the blazing logs; and of the little children who came out of the villages and stole through the woods to stare at them; and of one little maiden who had made so bold as to come and sit on John's knee, and had stroked his beard and chatted to him in French, and finally had

kissed him ere she went away. Sometimes they slept
on the ground with nothing but the bright stars overhead, and sometimes they made houses of leaves and
boughs, into which they crept at night, and were as
comfortable as could be.

But the chief part of the letter was taken up with
home affairs. John wanted to know all about his
Violet;—whether she was happy; what she did all
day; whether she went out to drive in her carriage;
if Fritz took good care of her; if Madam Adler
came often to see her. Had the good doctor been to
pay her a visit; was the canary well; did the poor
back ache much? And inside the envelope, folded
up carefully in a small piece of tissue-paper, were
some wild flowers gathered from under the trees
where they had bivouacked the night before. Violet
could put them into mother's Bible. The flowers
which she had given him were quite safe. He kept
them always in a little package near his heart, and
he loved to think of the words which Violet had
printed for him—" To meet again."

It is needless to say that Violet's eyes were full
before this letter was ended, and Madam Adler had
to speak quickly of the one which she must write to
him in answer, and of all the news she would have to
tell him—about her watch, and about the doctor's

visit, and how Ella's front tooth had fallen out, and she could no longer eat the hard ginger-bread nuts in the bakery.

Madam Adler promised to come over the next day to help her to write this letter, and having placed her mother's Bible on the bed beside her, she returned with an anxious heart to her own house to finish the closely-written page which lay hidden away in her pocket.

CHAPTER XVII.

THE next morning Violet waited with some impatience for the time to arrive at which Madam Adler had promised to come and help her to write her letter. She made Evelina put her desk upon the bed, and her mother's Bible; and she had on a snowy clean pinafore and a fresh purple bow tying up her hair.

Evelina looked very white this morning, and often when the child spoke to her she did not answer her. She went in and out of the room perpetually, and once or twice Violet heard her chattering in the street below in a low, excited voice; and when she did return, she did not look at Violet at all, but walked to the window and stared across at the house opposite.

"Is Madam Adler coming?" asked Violet a little wearily, as for the twentieth time she pushed the desk to one side, for the weight of it on the counterpane tired her so. "I heard the clock strike twelve ages ago."

"I do not see her coming," replied Evelina evasively.

" Is Fritz at the window ? "

" No."

" Or Ella ? "

" No."

"Couldst thou not go across and see if she will soon be here ? Do, Evelina, please."

Evelina turned slowly away from the window and went downstairs, while the little girl once more drew the desk near her, and, opening it, took out a sheet of paper and a pen.

But Evelina did not return for a long time, and Violet's head ached so much she had to lie back on her pillows. So the weary minutes dragged on, and there was no sound of any one coming. She drew out her watch and looked at it. It wanted but a quarter to one, and then it would be dinner-time, and the letter would surely be late for the post.

How fast the watch ticked, and yet how slowly the hands moved on. Her heart too was beating so loud and so fast she felt as if she were a part of the watch, and it made her more restless and impatient. So she put it back under her pillow and tried to lie quite still.

It was such a hot morning, and the sun was beating straight in on her bed. "If only Evelina would come back and draw down the blind," she murmured, for it was useless now to think of writing a letter before dinner-time.

There were ducks quacking somewhere down in the street, too, and making such a noise. When Evelina returned she must ask her to shut the window; and perhaps if she fell asleep for a few minutes her head would cease aching, and the sun would have moved away from her bed. All at once, just as she had pushed her desk quite away and lain down with her back to the window, she heard Fritz's voice raised quite loud and high in the room on the opposite side of the street; he was evidently calling out to some one in a tone of entreaty and dismay.

Violet with a sudden eagerness struggled upwards in her bed and listened.

"Mother, mother, look up! thou must look up! Father is not dead! father is not dead! Speak to Fritz!"

"What is it?" murmured Violet to herself with a sudden catch at her breath; "what is Fritz saying? —Oh! here is some one coming." For there was a sound of footsteps on the stairs, and then a low knock at the door.

It was the doctor. Violet recognized his kind good face with a start of joy, and stretched out her little white hands lovingly.

" So," he cried, looking first at her and then with surprise round the room. " How is this?—quite alone, little one ? "

" Yes, Evelina is gone out; she went across to call Madam Adler to come to me again."

" So," said the doctor again, his face growing somewhat graver as he looked earnestly at her. " I do not think that Madam Adler can come to see thee this morning. But first I must tell thee some good news: I have just heard that thy father is quite well."

" Yes ? " said Violet questioningly. " I also had a letter from my father;" and she held up an envelope which she had kept tightly pressed until now in her left hand.

" But mine was not a letter; it was a telegram."

" A telegram?" she repeated, puzzled and distressed.

" Yes, dearest child," said the doctor, taking her hand in his and half turning aside his head. " Thank God thy father is safe and well. I have made that sure for thee. But there has been a battle—a great battle; and our regiment was given the honour of being placed in the front; and some, of course, have been wounded; and some will never suffer any more;

and some are safe, and thy father is amongst those whom God has spared."

" My father ! " cried Violet excitedly ; " he has been in a battle, and he did not tell me so in his letter; and—and he is safe ! "

" Yes.   He could not have told thee in his letter. The battle was fought yesterday, and the news only came in last night."

" And is any one hurt ? " she cried, clasping the doctor's hand with her burning fingers.   " Is Fritz's father safe ? "

" I am afraid he has been very seriously hurt," he replied.

" He is not dead ? " gasped Violet.

" No, no ; not dead.   But it is uncertain whether he can recover."

" Poor, poor Fritz ! that is why he cried so loud this morning.   I heard him in my bed here calling to his mother."

" Just so.   Madam Adler is in terrible distress ; and Fritz, like a brave boy, is doing all he can to comfort her ; and when Fritz comes to see thee thou must be brave also, my Violet, and try to comfort him."

" Yes," she replied, nodding her head in assent, for words were growing difficult to speak, and large tears were rolling down her face. " I never thought of battles," she said pleadingly, as if in excuse for her tears.

" So much the better," said the doctor, pressing the little hot hand in his. " It is much pleasanter to think of peace."

" And soon there will be peace," she said, lifting up her dark, pitiful eyes to his face, heavy with tears.

" Yes, soon there will be peace," he replied, looking at her with a strange, long earnestness.

" And then I shall see father," she added softly, while through the troubled darkness of her eyes there came a slow sweet smile.

At this moment Evelina came into the room ; and the doctor hearing her enter, rose up to take his leave.

" Do not leave the child again to-day alone," he said in an undertone as he walked on towards the window where Evelina stood ; " and watch her carefully. People may come in and tell her things which may excite and pain her, and her little thread of life will not bear it. We must try to keep it going for a little longer. She is very weak this morning, and seems excited and restless."

" It is all about a letter to her father which she wishes Madam Adler to write for her ; and now the thing is impossible."

"Why cannot you write it for her, eh?"

"She will not have me to do it; no, not on any account," replied Evelina somewhat pettishly.

"Humph!" The doctor gazed out of the window for a moment, and then turning to her he said quickly,—

"You are very good to the child—careful, gentle, patient? These things are an absolute necessity."

"I do all I can to please her," said Evelina, blushing hotly under the doctor's earnest gaze. "But sick children are full of fancies."

"It is a privilege to nurse such a child. Had I not my own hands full of work, and the sick and the dying to think of, I should come and sit here day and night to watch by her and comfort her.—Eh, little one," he said, turning suddenly round and moving again towards the bed, "shall I come to-morrow morning early and write that letter for thee to thy father?"

"Oh, wilt thou?" cried Violet with a sudden access of unmeasured delight as she stretched out her arms gratefully. "That will be too lovely;—and thou canst tell him everything, and that Violet is quite well, and so—so—"

"Happy," suggested the doctor.

"Yes." (A faint blush.) "Yes, so happy waiting

for him to come home." The blush deepened as the truthful heart sought about to extricate itself.

"I understand," he said, taking both the little hands in his. "So happy when thou thinkest of father coming home, but often a little lonely and a little tired of waiting; and often the head aches, and one cannot be very happy when one's head is aching, can one?"

"Yes, that is it," replied Violet. "But I was not thinking of headaches, only sometimes—I am too tired; and then—" (she glanced towards Evelina nervously), "and then I am sorry if—"

"Exactly; so am I," cried the doctor laughing. "When I am too tired I feel as if I must take a stick and beat some one; and I am sure Evelina must be black and blue with all the bruises thou givest her. I should not at all like to receive a blow from this powerful wrist." The doctor stooped as he spoke and kissed the little hand he held in his. Violet laughed, and the rain of repentant tears was averted.

When the doctor left the room Evelina came and sat by Violet's bed. She drew her chair quite close, and speaking very gently to her she lifted the heavy desk off the counterpane and put it aside on the long walnut-wood chest, which, standing close to the bed, served as a kind of table.

"What a kind old fellow that doctor seems," she said presently. "He appears to be a great friend of thine."

"Yes," replied Violet softly; "father's friend and mother's, and now mine."

"Ah, so. And he has known thee all thy life?"

"Yes, all my life."

"And hast thou been sick always?"

"Yes, always." Violet sighed a little and moved somewhat restlessly on her pillow.

"And thy mother,—canst thou remember her?"

"Oh yes, quite well. She has not left me so very long. She slept there in that very room. She was too beautiful. All day long she sat with me, and I was always happy."

"And thy father—what is he like?"

"My father? Hast thou not seen him? He is, oh, so tall—almost up to the ceiling. He is the— but thou wilt see him for thyself, and then thou wilt know how splendid he is, and how good. When the war is over he will come home ever so fast to Violet."

"Without doubt," replied Evelina cheerfully. "And is he dark, or fair?"

"Quite dark."

"And thy mother—was she dark also?"

"Oh no. My mother, she is quite, quite fair. She

has yellow hair. I will show thee some of it." Violet put out her hand and drew over her mother's Bible, which lay on the counterpane. She touched it so reverently, and opened it with such a nervous thrill, that Evelina watched her movements with a growing interest.

Between the fly-leaves of the book there was a small package folded up in silver paper. The child opened this with nervous, trembling fingers, and revealed a lock of soft golden hair tied up with a black ribbon.

" And that is thy mother's hair ? How fine and soft and golden it is ! Why, it is almost the very same colour as mine. Let us see."

Evelina stretched out her hand to take it, but Violet drew back the book quickly; and then, blushing painfully at her own rudeness, shut up the little packet and closed the cover of the Bible.

" Ah, there is a page of thy book coming out now," cried Evelina, taking no apparent notice of her distress, and pointing to a loose leaf which stretched some distance beyond the cover.

" No, it is not possible !" She lifted up the book with a gesture of horror, but soon recovering herself said quickly,—" Ah, see, it is not out of the Bible. It is only the picture of the poor little hunchback. It fell out of its own cover, so I put it in here."

"A picture of what?" asked Evelina, looking curiously at the loose leaf which Violet had drawn from its resting-place.

"It is only a fairy tale," said Violet somewhat sadly as she placed the old faded print in Evelina's extended hand.

"How comical!" cried Evelina laughing. "The child has a face like an old man; but then all hunchbacks have got that kind of dried-up, wizened expression."

Violet bent her head low down over her mother's Bible to hide the sudden vivid colour which flooded all her face; but presently lifting up her head and seeing that Evelina was still staring curiously at the picture, she said very softly, almost in a whisper,—

"Thou knowest, dost thou not, that I am a little hunchback?"

"Oh, what folly!" (It was now Evelina's turn to grow confused and absolutely awkward.) "Why, thou little vain monkey, thou art fishing for compliments. It is useless for me to tell thee what thou art. Thou knowest well enough—'the sweet Violet of Edelsheim, the flower of all the town.'"

No responsive smile lit up Violet's face at this

sudden outburst of flattery. She only added, as if following out her own thoughts,—

"Fritz knows I am a hunchback, but he does not believe about the wings."

"What about the wings?"

"Dost thou not see in the picture there, low down on the page, where it is written, 'No more tears'? for dost thou not see God gave the little hunchback wings, and she flew quite away with the angels up, up to heaven."

"Oh, yes, of course," cried Evelina. "I have read the story in another book, only it was about a boy. He had, oh, such a dreadful hump on his back, so ugly, people could not bear to look at him; or if they did they made faces at him and pointed their fingers at him, and even his own mother was ashamed. But all the time there were beautiful golden wings folded up inside his hump; and one day when—when—;" Evelina hesitated a little and pinched up the frilling of her cuff nervously.

"Yes, what?—go on," cried Violet. Evelina looked up. The child's eyes shone with a purple light of joy; her face was radiant, her lips trembled. "Go on, go on."

"Well, one day when he was out walking in the street, a wicked, cruel boy threw a stone at him—

a large, heavy stone—and it struck him on the back."

"Go on," cried Violet, clutching Evelina's wrist with her burning little hand. "God helped him, I am sure."

"Yes, God helped him; for when all the people cried out and ran to him suddenly, there came a great light all round him, so that they could not see where he lay, and there were angels all round about him comforting him; and then out of his poor aching shoulders there sprang up all at once two great shining wings, and the angels whispered something in his ears, and he stretched his wings wide out, and away he flew with them right up to heaven; and God opened the gates and took him in, and he was at rest."

"Yes, quite at rest; and he too had no more tears, and he was quite, quite happy," said Violet. "And this is all true, is it not, Evelina?"

Evelina caught one glimpse of the little quivering face, and she replied quickly,—

"Without doubt; at least it is just as I read it in the book."

"It was not a fairy tale?"

"No, certainly not."

"Evelina, come closer. There, put thy arms round

my neck." Violet pressed her little burning lips on Evelina's cheek. " I will never be cross with thee any more—never, never. I will try to love thee better every day.—And all the poor sick hunchbacks have wings, have they not ; and I, too, I shall have wings ? "

" Oh yes, beautiful shining wings." In Evelina's own throat there was a catch now, and she breathed painfully. " There, let me settle thy pillows, and try and rest a bit ; it will do thee good to sleep awhile."

" Yes, I am so tired ; but that story thou toldest me is too, too lovely." She loosened her arms from Evelina's neck and lay back with a long contented sigh.

" Where shall I put this Bible, darling ? "

" On the chest, please ; or stay, it is better to put it inside. Open the lid and lay it down in the corner quite close to my bed."

Evelina raised the cover, as she was told, and placed the book in the spot indicated by Violet.

" Take care that thou dost not crush the hat. Just lift the muslin and see."

Evelina lifted a long strip of muslin which lay all along the inside of the chest. In the corner next the bed there lay a large Leghorn hat, trimmed with pale blue ribbon and forget-me-nots.

" Ah, how beautiful ! Whose hat is it ? " she asked, stooping quickly to examine it.

"It is my mother's. She always wore it on Sundays. And father put it by there with all her other clothes when—when—; but please cover it up and shut the box."

Evelina closed the lid very slowly, her eyes to the last moment dwelling on the forget-me-nots and the trimming of pale blue satin.

"Lovely!" she said again to herself as she shut down the cover.

"Yes, lovely!" murmured Violet, whose eyelids were already closing; "and when Violet has wings mother will be standing there, beside God, waiting for her."

"Poor child!" said Evelina, turning and looking compassionately at the little faded face on the pillow; "she has but one idea, and that is heaven." Then crossing the room and opening the door of the inner apartment, she walked gently over to the glass which stood on the dressing-table, and gazed at herself for a long time in the mirror. "I am sure I should look lovely in that hat," she said presently. "I have just the complexion for forget-me-nots, and besides, my hair is just the same colour as the lock she showed me." And then taking up her knitting from the table, she returned to Violet's room and sat down in the window to work.

CHAPTER XVIII.

SORROWFUL TIDINGS.

THE next morning the doctor came early, and, true to his promise, acted as scribe for Violet. Such a long letter as was despatched to poor John, full of all the little scraps of news that Violet had been treasuring up for ever so long, and a few leaves of the ivy which grew up the side of the house and in at the window where she generally sat, and one yellow feather which had dropped out of the canary bird's wing. Violet felt quite elated when the letter was finished, and the doctor himself carried it off to the post, leaving her smiling, with eyes bright with pleasure and cheeks just a little flushed by the unusual exertion.

When the doctor was gone she insisted on being lifted up and placed as usual in the window. Evelina was surprised at the energy she showed in all her movements, and the weary time of her dressing went on with fewer sighs than usual.

It was not until she was actually seated in her old chair in the embrasure that she seemed for the first time to realize the terrible trouble that had come upon her friends in the house opposite.   She had been so busy thinking of her father and of the letter which was to go to him, that she had not taken in all the sorrow that had fallen on the town and its inhabitants; but she could not sit long at the window this morning and not see or hear something of it.   It seemed to her, after a little time, that all the people in Edelsheim were weeping.

There were women standing at Madam Adler's door wringing their hands, and others with aprons to their eyes sobbing.   Many of them had slips of paper in their hands which they gazed at every moment, and then burst out crying afresh.   Even the policeman, as he passed down the street opposite, had tears in his eyes, and as he tried to smile up at her window Violet saw how they fell on the breast of his coat.

"What are they all crying for in the street below?" she asked plaintively, as Evelina came out of the inner room and sat down in the window seat opposite her: "is Fritz's father so very, very ill, or what is it?"

"It is not only for him they are weeping, poor creatures," cried Evelina, gazing earnestly after the policeman, who was slowly pacing down the street with his head bent upon his chest. " They have all suffered, poor souls. There is not one in Edelsheim that has not lost a friend, or a brother, a father, or a husband, or a lover. The regiment was in the very front of the battle, and the men were mowed down like grass ; at least so the paper says."

" What paper ?"

" The newspaper : but the doctor said thou wert on no account to see it ; indeed I ought not to speak to thee of such things at all, only one must answer plain questions when they are put to one.—Oh, here comes the little Ella and her brother ; they are crossing the street, and they will bring thee all the news."

Violet turned quickly round, for her eyes had been fixed with an ever increasing horror on Evelina's face, and now she just caught a glimpse of Ella's fair hair floating behind her as she passed under the overhanging eaves of the window.

In a moment more both children had burst into the room, Ella a little in advance of Fritz, who was quite breathless and red in his endeavours to keep pace with her, and had his hand tightly locked in the gathers of her dress, by which he vainly tried to hold her back.

" Hast thou heard, Violet ?" cried Ella, her voice

raised almost to a scream as she endeavoured to be the first to tell the news,—" hast thou heard that father has lost his leg, one whole leg ?   It is quite true : first they shot it off, and then they cut it off, and now he is in the hospital.   And the policeman's son has both his arms shot off him ; and the father of the orange-girl is dead, and she was screaming all the morning on the steps of the chapel, and no oranges in her basket at all."

" Silence, you little dunderhead,". cried Fritz, shaking Ella so violently by her skirt that she was forced for a moment to pause and resent his rudeness ; " did not mother tell thee this morning that thou wert not to frighten Violet with all these stories ?"

" But are they true ?" asked Violet eagerly.

" Yes, quite true," echoed Ella.

Violet still looked towards Fritz for confirmation.

" Yes, they are quite true," he said gravely ; " but thy father is safe.   Mother said so ; she had a telegram from him this morning."

" A telegram ?"

" Well, yes.   A message to say father was going on well, and to give thee his love."

" His love," echoed Violet in a whisper.

" And loads and loads of people are dead," continued Ella, who had not half exhausted her store of news; "and the little man who used to sell the peppermint sticks has had his whole head blown off. His wife says it is not a bit true, and she wanted to go off in a cart this morning to look for him, only the doctor would not let her. Mother said the poor woman's head was gone; so then, you see, they would neither of them have heads, I suppose; and would not that be rather funny, Violet?"

Evelina tittered a little, and went into the next room to hide her laughter; but Fritz grew very red, and said angrily, "The little donkey! she does not know what she talks about, only picking up what other people say."

"I don't pick up what other people say. I heard every word, and lots more," rejoined Ella stoutly; but still she blushed at Fritz's reproof, and shuffled her shoulders along the wall uneasily.

"And is thy father very sick? will he come home soon?" asked Violet, whose face and lips had been gradually whitening as the children's talk went on.

"Ah, that I cannot tell thee. Mother says it will be a long time before he can move at all, and then he will have to get crutches."

"And must he always walk with crutches, always, always?" asked Violet, whose mind was only gradually opening up to all the sadness of the occasion.

"Yes, always," replied Fritz; "for, of course, he could not walk on one leg."

"I can hop on one leg," observed Ella from the corner into which she had been gradually retreating. "This morning, when I heard all about father, I hopped six times up and down the kitchen and never put my hand on anything."

"And can thy father never bake any more bread, nor stand any more at the door in the evening and kiss hands up to me?"

"That I do not know.   He will stand, perhaps, in the bakery and look on; and then, thou knowest, he can have a chair put down in the doorway, and he can see thee from there.—O Ella, canst thou not keep still?"

For Ella had now emerged from her corner near the stove, and with the handle of the little stove-brush planted under her arm, was prancing up and down the floor with one leg drawn up behind her and the other coming down at intervals with tremendous thumps on the floor.

"Do keep still," cried Fritz again.

But Ella, who had sat all day long silent and miserable in the house opposite, was now flushed with the excitement of freedom both of limb and speech, and up and down the room she hopped and bounded with glowing cheeks and flying hair, crying out, "See how I can hop!" until at last the brush-stick slipped with a sudden jerk from under her arm, and she came crash down on the floor on her face.

"Ha, ha! that comes from pretending to have only one leg," shouted Fritz, half laughing himself at the catastrophe. But when he picked up poor Ella and found that her lip was cut and swelled, and her little fat elbow all scraped and bleeding, too, he carried her over in his arms to a chair and kissed her a hundred times. It was all, however, of no avail. Ella, it is true, made no sound whatever for a moment or two, and Violet, quite terrified, leaned forward in her chair anxiously.

But Ella was only waiting to recover her breath: her nerves had been strained to the highest pitch, poor child, and now with almost a convulsive struggle a piercing cry burst forth, loud and long, and terrifying to hear. Evelina came rushing out of the inner room, and snatching the child from Fritz's arms, without listening to explanation or remonstrance, she carried her down the stairs and quickly across the street to her mother. Fritz sprang up to follow, but looking round at Violet's pale face, he paused and hesitated.

"I will stay with thee till she comes back," he said

comfortingly, and he returned and stood by her side, though his lips and hands trembled with the passion he strove to repress.

They could hear poor Ella's cries all the way up the stairs and long after she entered the little sitting-room opposite. They saw her mother take her upon her knee, and press her head against her bosom, and dry her eyes softly with her handkerchief, and wipe the blood from her lip. And then Fritz saw Evelina come out of the door again; but she did not cross the street or look up at their window as he expected she would do, but instead she walked for some distance along the narrow pavement until she met the police-man, who was slowly returning on his beat.

" Pah !" cried Fritz, shooting out his lips with a motion of the supremest contempt, " she is a sly old fox, and I hate her."

" Whom ?" asked Violet, whose mind had wandered far away, and whose hand was resting wearily on the cover of her mother's Bible.

" Evelina," cried Fritz stoutly ; " she is a vain old chattering pea-hen."

" Ah no, thou must not say so, Fritz."

" Why not ? she does not care one straw for thee."

" Yes, yes, she does ; she has told me such lovely things."

" What about ? "

" Ah, about a poor sick boy. It was not a fairy tale ; it was quite true. He was a poor little hunchback like me, and God gave him wings, beautiful silver wings ; and some one threw a stone at him, and all at once he stretched out his wings, and angels came to meet him, and he went right up to heaven ;—and this story is true."

Fritz coloured violently and made no reply. He looked a moment into Violet's eyes and then gazed nervously aside. Presently he came over to her chair and put his arm round her neck.

" No, no, it is not true," he cried in a sudden anguish ; " it must not be true ; I do not want thee to have wings. Thou must get well. I do not want thee to die and go away and leave me."

" To die ? " said Violet with a little gasp ; " ah no, I do not want to die ; only mother said when I had wings I should have no more pain and no more tears. And now thou art crying, Fritz, and I do not like to see it."

" I cannot help crying," sobbed Fritz.

" Then thou hadst better take up thy cap and go away," said Evelina somewhat sharply from the doorway ; " we have had tears enough in this room for one day."

Fritz rose up proudly and took his cap from the table at the foot of the bed.

" And when thou talkest· to the policeman next time," continued Evelina in the same unpleasant tone, " thou mayest find some other subject more interesting to him than to talk about me, and tell tales of—"

" I told no tales," cried Fritz hotly ; " he asked me wert thou very good to his little friend Violet, that was all."

" Well, and what didst thou say ?"

" I said nothing ; I did not answer him. I went into the house and shut the door."

" That was the most unkind thing thou couldst have done. It was worse than telling tales."

" I will be kinder next time," cried Fritz with a sudden spirit ; " I will tell him everything."

" Thou hast nothing to tell," screamed Evelina down the staircase.

" Ha, ha !" laughed Fritz ; " ask the looking-glass, —it sees more of thee than any one else."

" Little villain ! he shall not see much more of us," said Evelina angrily, as she shut the door and came back into the room. " The children at Gützberg would not dare to speak to me like that ; they have better manners.—Wilt thou have thy dinner now ?" she added more quietly, as she caught the look of weary pain and deep distress on Violet's face.

" No, thank you ; I could not eat, I am so tired ; please let me go back to bed."

Evelina undressed the child in silence ; she was not cross, but her cheeks burned and she seemed engrossed in her own thoughts.

Violet was not long in bed before she fell asleep. She was very tired, and she slept heavily. When she woke again the afternoon was almost spent and the room was empty. She raised herself a little on her pillows and looked about her. The door of the inner room was slightly ajar, and she leaned forward to see if any one was there. She could just catch a glimpse of Evelina's figure. She was standing opposite the mirror and was trying something on her head.

" It is mother's hat," gasped Violet ; " I see the blue ribbons."

At this moment Evelina turned round quickly, and catching a glimpse of the child's face, she shut the door with a snap.

CHAPTER XIX.

A BRIGHT PROSPECT.

IT seemed to Violet, as the long autumn days went by, and she sat in the old place in the window, that the town was changed. All the people who went by in the street were dressed in black; very few smiled as they looked up at her, though they kissed their hands as usual and nodded their heads. The basket-bell seldom rang now; and, worst of all, Fritz never came to see her.

It was not that Evelina had carried her threat into execution; but, alas! Fritz had got the hooping-ccugh, and the doctor had forbidden him to enter Violet's house. It would be fatal to the child, he said, to catch such an illness; and one must remember not only her weakness, but also the great love of poor John away at the war, who was ever, day and night, thinking of his darling, and wondering whether God would spare her to him until his return.

So the days dragged on somewhat heavily, and

Violet grew very weary. No air seemed to come down from the hill far away. The little children who went on expeditions to gather nuts were nearly all dressed in black, and they did not come back singing and dancing as they used to do. Evelina once brought in an apronful of nuts and poured them into Violet's lap; and Ella, too, came bouncing in one afternoon with an old cap of Fritz's full to the brim with the choicest hazels; but Violet had no fancy for them, though she kissed Ella and thanked Evelina for remembering her.

"When father comes home," she said to Ella, "then he will take me in my carriage to the hill, first to see mother, and then all the way up the hill; the nuts will not be gone by that time?" she said questioningly.

"I will take thee out to-morrow to the hill, if thou choosest," said Evelina, looking round towards the corner of the room where the carriage stood covered over by a rug; "it would brighten thee up a bit, and Miss Ella could come too if she liked."

"Yes, yes!" cried Ella, jumping about wildly and flinging her arms around Violet's neck. "Come, come, come, come to-morrow and gather nuts with Ella!"

"I should like to go with father first," said Violet

nervously, for the temptation was great; "and my back aches so, I should be frightened."

"Thy back will not ache less for waiting," observed Evelina shortly.

"No, not one bit less," urged Ella with the broadest smile of satisfaction on her face.

"And as to waiting for thy father," continued Evelina, "goodness knows when he will be back again; the leaves and nuts and all may be off the trees before the war is over."

"Yes; leaves and nuts and all," echoed Ella; "and mother says perhaps the snow will be on the ground before our soldiers come home, and battles and battles and battles. And do you know they tumble all the dead horses into great big holes—fifteen great horses into one hole; and one great enormous shell which a man shot out of a gun, it first went through a house, and then it went through a garden, and then it went through a wall, and then it went through a woman who was baking a cake, and at last it went through a steeple, and down tumbled the whole church, and every one was killed; and was not that a grand shot, Violet?"

Ella spread out her arms triumphantly and laughed in concert with Evelina, who shrieked in the corner.

"The policeman said it was not one bit true; but he is a mouldy old fellow," cried Ella excitedly; "he was never in no battles, only marching up and down and up and down. He gave me a flower for thee, Violet, yesterday, and as I was standing in the street it fell in the gutter, and the water carried it off in one moment under the stones."

" A flower ? for me ? "

" Yes ; he had it in his hand, and he said, ' Give this to my little friend in the window up there ;' and while I was looking ever so high up trying to see thee, down fell the flower in the water, and away it goes. But what harm? it was only a little violet," cried Ella, drawing close to Violet with eyes full of a great mystery.

" What is it ? "

" Fritz found it out himself the other day and showed it to me and to mother."

" What ? " again asked Violet, her eyes gazing eagerly into the little face before her.

" Violets have got humps on their backs ; and thou —thou—art a violet too, and thou hast a hump on thy back; and is not that funny ? "

" Hush ! " cried Evelina, catching Ella by the skirt of her dress and trying to draw her back from Violet's chair ; " such talk is not allowed in this room."

" Oh yes, let her tell me ; I love to hear what Fritz says about the violets."

" What a strange child she is!" cried Evelina to herself as she let go the skirt.

" Go on," said Violet anxiously ; " what more did Fritz say ? "

" He had seven violets in his hand. He spread them all out on the table and counted them, for he had sent me with a whole penny to the shop, and only got back seven flowers. The woman had no flowers in her shop, only lovely yellow wreaths with writing on them to hang on dead people's graves; and when I brought one back to Fritz he was mad angry, and said he would not send thee over such a thing for all the world. He called me a blockhead, and said thy father was not dead, but quite alive and well, and it was no use ; and so the woman gave the violets."

" Yes," said Violet somewhat faintly.

" And Fritz was so angry. He spread them all out on the table, and was going to chop off all their heads with a knife, when he found out about the humps ; and then he called mother up from the bakery and showed them to her."

" And what did she say ? " asked Violet, deeply interested in Ella's recital.

" Fritz asked was that why they called thee Violet, because thou also hast a hump ? and mother said,

'Hush, foolish boy.' Violet was like a little angel when she was born, and soon she would be an angel again. And then Fritz got his penknife and cut open all the humps, to see what was in them; and there wasn't anything to see, only things all folded up, and quite shining."

" Ah," murmured Violet faintly.

"And then Fritz gave a great cough, and away flew all the violets off the table—heads and tails, and humps and all; and mother had to hold Fritz by both the hands, for he coughed as if his head would have fallen off too."

Ella laughed heartily at the recollection, and letting go Violet's dress clambered up into the window, where, kneeling on the window-sill, she seized upon some of the wooden animals ranged along the ledges, and began with infinite pains to make the camel try to kiss the elephant. "Only I don't know where the elephant keeps his mouth," she said plaintively.

By-and-by she ceased playing and fell to singing, her round face pressed against the window-frame, and her eyes looking out towards the hill.

Evelina put down her knitting and listened. The child had the sweetest voice in all Edelsheim—clear, fresh, and true. She sang unconsciously a hymn about green pastures and lambs who followed their

Shepherd by the side of still waters, and whom, when weary, he carried in his bosom tenderly and full of care.

Evelina looked across at Violet to express her admiration and amazement at the beauty and pathos of the child's voice; but Violet did not see her, for her eyes were fixed on the little cap beside her filled with the fresh hazel-nuts, with their pale green leaves, and rich with the odour of the trees which grew on the hill yonder still hanging about them. A great longing was beginning to fill her soul—to go out like all the other children and see the woods and the squirrels and the boughs laden with their fruit; to see the cattle and the fields and the little waterfall close by the road, at the foot of which Fritz had told her one could always find lovely damp moss with leaves which looked like trees. She had some of these leaves put away in mother's Bible, and she would like to see them and gather them for herself.

And now so deep was her reverie that she did not even notice Ella's descent from the window-sill, and was scarcely conscious of the parting kiss, given in some haste as Fritz had signalled to Ella to return home at once, and had held out to her view a tempting cake full of currants, and covered over with pink sugar.

When Ella was gone Evelina rose up to prepare the dinner; but her attention was once more drawn to the child's deep reverie, and to the earnest gaze fixed so immovably upon the cap full of green nuts which rested on her knees.

"Well, Violet, what art thou thinking of, with thy great big eyes so wide open?" she asked, turning round with the wooden bread-plate in her hand. "Art thou searching for a wood-fairy amongst the leaves?"

"No; I was thinking."

"Thinking of what?"

"I was thinking of the hill, and of the carriage father made for me, and of what thou wert saying a few minutes ago about—about—about going to the hill."

"Yes, certainly; why not? We will put thee in thy carriage after dinner, and away we shall go all the way up the hill; and we shall have rare fun. I shall send across after dinner for Miss Ella, and she shall push and I will pull; and then, when we are there, we can pack all the nuts into the foot of the carriage, and then we will cover thee all over with boughs, and every one will say as we return, 'Oh, look at our little Violet hidden among the sweet green leaves.'"

Evelina was in her best mood to-day ; and, besides, when she looked into the child's eyes she always felt a stirring in her heart, like the good seed trying to thrust itself up amongst the tares and follies of her vain and wavering nature.

Violet could not eat much of the dinner Evelina had got ready for her, though it was hot and tempting enough.   Evelina had a taste for cookery, and the meals were always well and skilfully prepared.

To-day her mind was too disturbed to be conscious almost of what she was eating.   This expedition to the hill was full of an excitement which choked and stifled her.   To be out in the fresh air, to hear the birds sing, to see the trees waving, to watch the children gathering nuts; perhaps they even might hold down some of the boughs close enough to her carriage, so that she might gather some herself !   And then only to think what a letter she could write to her father! how rejoiced he would be to think that his carriage had been used at last, and that the expedition to the hill had been such a happy one.

Evelina ate her own dinner very happily, and tried to induce Violet to do the same.   She laughed and chatted, and was herself quite elated at the thought of the expedition.   The little girl grew more and more excited as Evelina described all the things they would see and all the people they would meet. Her eyes glowed and her cheeks burned, and when the dinner was over she watched with an ever-increasing anxiety the preparations which Evelina began to make for their expedition.

The carriage was drawn out from its covering; the cushions were dusted; pillows with clean frilled covers over them were placed carefully on the cushions to support Violet's back and shoulders. Then on the rail at the back was hung a basket for the nuts; and on the foot Evelina threw a scarlet shawl of her own, which gave a bright and glowing finish to it all.

"Evelina, thou art too kind," cried Violet, stretching out her arms suddenly. "I will tell father—I will tell everybody—how good thou art to me."

Evelina returned the child's embrace warmly, blushing a little as she did so.

"Ah, if so, thou wilt be better than Master Fritz yonder," she cried, looking quickly across at the house opposite. "A nice character he gave of me to the policeman, who will not so much as look at me now if I meet him in the street. But what do I care?— not one hazel-nut for him or his long sallow face, the old stick-in-the-mud. He asks every one as many questions about thee as if he were thy father."

"He is my friend," said Violet nervously, as she heard the thrill of anger in Evelina's tones.

"Bah! I suppose because he walks up and down the street, and kisses hands to thee now and again as he goes by, he reckons himself thy friend—much more of a friend than those who take care of thee all day and all night. But what is the use of talking? It is not of him we are thinking, but of the lovely ride we are going to have to-day to the woods. Let me see now;—where is thy hat? and thou wilt want some little coat, I suppose, to put over thy dress."

"I have no hat," replied Violet, looking up with suddenly clouded eyes—" no hat, and no coat."

"How is that?—neither hat nor coat?"

"Father said he would buy me a hat and cloak when he took me out in my carriage; but he is not here now. O Evelina, cannot I go in the carriage as Ella often goes in Fritz's wooden cart? Or Ella, perhaps, would lend me a hat. Do go across and see if thou canst find me one somewhere." It seemed to Violet as if some great impediment had suddenly started up in the path of her promised happiness.

"I need not go to trouble Madam Adler about hats. I could put something better on thy head than anything she could lend thee," said Evelina with a

little laugh. "Why, a beggar child in Edelsheim
would not pick Miss Ella's hat out of the gutter."

Violet did not hear this remark about Edelsheim or
her little friend Ella. A thought had suddenly come
into her head, and she was struggling with herself
how best she could make it known to her companion.

"Evelina !"

"Well, what is it ? I suppose thou art too grand to
wear one of my hats ?"

"No, no; but I have thought of something. I
would like to wear mother's hat, which is in the box."

"What! the splendid Leghorn with the blue silk
ribbons ? Impossible."

"Why ?" asked Violet, colouring violently as she
met the astonished eyes of Evelina. "It has forget-
me-nots on it, and I would love to wear it—oh, this
one day. Do not shake thy head so, Evelina. Father
said that by-and-by, when I was big, I might wear it."

"Thy father, of course, can give thee leave to do
what he likes when he is here; but to wear such a hat
to go to the hill, the very thought of it is ridiculous."

"But mother would love me to wear it. She gave
me always what I asked for," pleaded Violet with
tear-choked earnestness.

"And that is just why thou art such a little spoiled
brat, who must have everything thine own way.

Then let us talk no more about it.   The hat would be destroyed if it were crushed up against the pillows, the brim would be broken; and the dust and leaves and dirt off the trees would ruin the trimming.   Wait some day until I take thee to church, and then—"

"To church!" cried Violet, stretching out her hands suddenly, and uttering a cry of joy.

"Yes, yes; why not?   We can draw thee there some day in the carriage, and I can carry thee inside in my arms."

"And I shall see where mother is asleep.   Is it not so, Evelina?"

"Yes, yes.   Now dry up thy tears, and think of the nuts and the trees, and all the fun we are going to have."

Violet drew a deep sigh of relief, and turned her eyes once more towards the carriage.   Her heart was too full for any words as she wiped the tears off her cheeks and pinafore, and gazed with interest at Evelina, who, having finished setting the room in order, began to prepare herself for the expedition by putting a little muslin tippet on her shoulders, tied up with blue bows; and the daintiest white frilled cap upon her head, which sat just far enough back to show the pretty golden curls which clustered round her forehead coaxingly.

"Now, little lovebird," she said, turning with her pleasantest smile towards the sick child, whose eyes, she could see, were following all her movements with an almost ardent admiration,—"now I am off to look for a little hat for thyself. I saw one in a shop yesterday, just beside the flower-shop, and it is just the very thing for thee. It is made of brown straw, shady, and yet not too large. I shall not be a moment away."

"Thou art too good, Evelina," cried Violet eagerly. "And if thou seest the policeman tell him that I am going out to-day in my carriage. He will be glad, I know, to hear that, for he is my friend ; and I will say to him how good thou art to me."

"Yes, yes," shouted Evelina, turning briskly down the stairs; "if I see him I shall tell him." And Violet, leaning back in her chair, folded her arms on her lap and looked across at the top of the green hill, in whose cool shadows she hoped so soon to be resting.

Evelina was not very long away. She returned blushing and smiling with a pretty brown hat in her hand having a wreath of yellow buttercups twisted round its crown.

"There, darling," she cried, placing it on Violet's head, "is not that lovely ? The woman in the shop nearly wept for joy when she heard it was for thee ;

and she chose this wreath for thee herself. She
actually refused to take any money for it, not a
penny, though I said if thy father were at home he
would insist on paying her. 'Ah, that is another
thing,' she said, pinning the flowers round the hat
so tastefully. 'I would accept twenty shillings this
moment to know he were safe at home.' Was not
that good of her?" asked Evelina, tilting the hat a
little back on Violet's head. "We must not quite
cover up thy face for all that, my angel," she added
laughing, "or what would the old policeman say?"

"The policeman!" cried Violet eagerly; "why, didst
thou see him?"

"Ah, now indeed I have some news for thee. I
met him just at the corner by the flower-shop, and
told him all about that promised drive to the hill
this afternoon; and what dost thou think? He said
if we could wait a while, until his duty was over, he
would come with us there himself, and that he would
rather draw thee one mile in thy little cart than the
king himself in his state coach. I laughed at the old
silly. As if he could draw the king one step, let alone
the heavy state coach! But he is, after all, a good
soul, for he nearly wept with joy at the news that
thou wert going out, and asked so many questions
about the carriage and the cushions that I thought

I should never get home. So now I have been across and told little Ella that we shall not be ready just yet awhile; and her mother is delighted at the delay, for the child had just spilt a whole bottle of ink over her dress and pinafore and stockings, and she will require time to make her neat again. She had been crying, too, poor little wretch! for her eyes were sticking out like crabs' eyes; and Fritz had her on his knee, and was cramming bon-bons into her mouth."

"Good old Fritz," said Violet softly.

"Oh, good indeed! thou shouldst have heard all he said, and the names he called me; because why? he thinks thou shouldst not go to the hill without him. But his mother told him that was folly, as the summer would be over before he had done coughing. And then he talked a lot of rubbish about the doctor, and asking his leave; but bah! who listens to such a chattering magpie?"

"Poor Fritz! father promised him that he should be the first to draw me in the carriage to the hill," said Violet, half speaking to herself; but Evelina, who had grown angry, caught the words, and said quickly,—

"Very good. Let Fritz be the first to draw thee to the hill! the policeman and I can well afford to wait for such an honour." Then seeing that the child had quite failed to take in the meaning of her cutting words, she added in a more kindly tone,—

"See now, it wants nearly two hours to the time when the policeman can come here, and—"

"Two hours!" interrupted Violet, with almost a cry of disappointment.

"Yes, two hours; and so much the better for thee, for now the sun is so hot it would just bake thee into a little pie. There was a child yesterday, Master Fritz said, who went to the hill and got such a headache from standing in a cornfield beside the river that last night they thought it was going to die."

"Oh," said Violet thoughtfully;—she was thinking of the story in the Bible which Fritz had told her one time long ago. "And is it well now, Evelina?"

"I do not know; I did not ask. The policeman can tell thee. He is not such a bad old fellow, after all. He is going to bring out cakes, and strawberries and cream, and a kettle, and I don't know what else, and we are to have tea under the trees. Is not that lovely?"

"Lovely! too, too lovely!" replied Violet, her eyes kindling with a speechless joy. "And perhaps, Evelina, I shall hear the nightingales singing in the woods. Mother used to walk down there with father in the evenings long ago to listen, and once she had me in her arms—father told me so; but then I was only a very small baby. And shall I see glow-worms, too, and those little mice which have wings ? "

"Yes, yes, everything," replied Evelina, who was busy buttoning on a pair of very dainty boots : "we shall have a delicious evening, that is certain. And I would have thee go asleep now and think no more about it, and when thou awakest the two hours will be gone, and we shall lift thee straight away into thy carriage, and then hurrah for the hill! Why, thou wilt feel just like a bird escaped from its cage ; and when once thou hast stretched thy wings and flown to the woods, I reckon we shall have pretty hard work to keep thee in the house any longer."

" My wings ! " echoed Violet in a tone of such concentrated interest that Evelina looked up startled and astonished ; " when shall I have wings ? "

" Little goose," replied the girl, turning away her head suddenly from the sight of those pleading eyes ; " how can I tell thee ? Perhaps we shall cheat thee after all of thy wings, when we get thee out into the fresh air and the fields ; and then what will thy father think when he comes home ? "

" I do not understand what thou meanest," said Violet plaintively.

" Never mind what I mean: wings are all very well, no doubt, for birds and things that cannot walk;

(789)   14

but fine fat arms and legs are better still. Ah, thou
shouldest see thy cousins at Gützberg; they are something like children. I would not drag one of those
fat things to the hill in thy carriage, not for all thou
couldst give me."

"But thou rememberest the little sick girl in the
book, dost thou not, Evelina?" asked Violet, puzzled
and anxious.

"In what book?"

Violet placed her hand on the spotted cover beside
her on the table. "The picture is in mother's Bible,"
she said softly.

"Oh yes, to be sure, I remember all about it; but
we need not think about such sad things to-day. Go
to sleep now, and I will draw this blind down beside
thee and darken the room a bit."

As Evelina stretched up her arms to reach the
tassel of the narrow blind beside Violet's chair she
caught her by her apron and said earnestly,—

"But thou, Evelina, thou believest that I shall have
wings?"

"Of course I do."

"And will it be soon?"

"Oh, how can I tell? before the winter, I daresay."

"Before the winter?" repeated Violet reflectively;
"that is not long to wait."

"What a strange child thou art!" cried Evelina, putting her arms suddenly round Violet's neck and kissing her; "why art thou in such a hurry to leave us all? Is not Evelina good to thee?"

"Oh yes, too good; only my back aches so, and the wings are so long coming."

Evelina looked at the little white face turned up to her so wistfully, and said in her softest voice, "Pray to God, darling, for thy wings. He can give them to thee when he likes."

"Yes, I do pray every day, and Fritz too; and thou, Evelina, thou also wilt ask God every morning and every evening when thou sayest thy prayers, wilt thou not?" Evelina suddenly flushed scarlet and turned away her face from the earnest pleading eyes. "Wilt thou not, Evelina?"

"Yes, yes, of course; only do not let us talk any more about wings. Thou wilt be too tired for thy drive. Lie back on thy pillows now and dream of strawberries and cream, and thy friend the old policeman sitting with thee under the trees on the hill, and all the care he will take of thee, and of the long letter we must write by-and-by to thy father of all we have seen and done."

CHAPTER XX.

ALL ALONE.

IT was the sound of a cannon fired from the fort just across the river that woke Violet from the sleep into which she had fallen, and in which she had lain now peacefully resting for the last two hours.

She did not often sleep so heavily in the day-time, but this afternoon she had been so excited and restless that her little body had felt quite worn out, and she had scarcely lain back on her pillows before a most delicious sleep had overtaken her.

She had dreamt, too, such a lovely dream: a dream that she was out gathering flowers in a wide meadow at the foot of the hill—beautiful blue forget-me-nots and the yellow narcissus; and that morning, beside her and holding her hand, all dressed in white, with beautiful silver wings, was another child whom she seemed to know at once to be the little girl the doctor had told her of, who in the spring time, when the flowers were starting up and the larks were beginning to sing, had suddenly escaped, like a bird from its cage, and spreading her wings had flown right up to God.

But now, in the dream, she was in the meadow with Violet, holding her hand and leading her along, and pointing out to her the beautiful flowers which were growing here and there through the grass. And Violet wondered even in her dream how it was that she had no pain in her shoulders, and that her feet seemed to carry her along so easily and swiftly over the meadows—sometimes, indeed, they did not seem to touch the ground at all, but only to skim over the heads of the tall grasses; and a delicious breeze was blowing down from the hill and wafting her along towards the spot where the forget-me-nots grew thickest, and where the sweet-scented jonquils stood up so pure and white in their beauty.

And while she was stooping and gathering the blue flowers which she loved the best, she thought she heard a voice calling to her a long way off down the meadow—a very gentle voice, which at first sounded as if Aunt Lizzie were calling to her; but the little girl touched her on the shoulder and said,—

" Violet, dost thou not hear thy mother calling to thee ? "

" My mother ! where ? " and then remembering

suddenly that her mother was dead, she said very sadly, "It cannot be my mother, for she is not here any longer; she is up in heaven with the angels, and I cannot go to her until God has given me wings."

"Ah, dost thou not know that this is heaven, and that thou hast wings?"

Then Violet, looking up suddenly, saw that the air was full of shining figures flitting to and fro across the sky; and there was a shining hill on which stood a great white throne, and on the steps of the throne the Lord Jesus was standing with a little lamb in his arms; and Violet suddenly felt herself rising up into the air like the angels, and soon she was flying swiftly across the meadow in the direction of the throne, flying, flying ever faster, that she might meet the good Lord Jesus whom she loved so much, and see the lamb that he had folded so closely to his breast.

At last she came to the foot of the shining steps, and the good Lord Jesus was standing there waiting for her with a smile on his face; and she said to him very softly, "Dear Lord Jesus, show me the little lamb whom thou art carrying in thy bosom." And the Lord Jesus answered her, in a low, sweet voice, "Dost thou not know this is the little Violet from

Edelsheim ? She has fallen asleep, and I am going to lay her in her mother's arms."

And Violet saw then that it was a little sick maiden that he carried so lovingly ; and she stretched up that she might see the little girl's face. And when she did see it, it was quite white, and there were tears upon the cheeks, though the eyes were closed.

But even while she was looking at it wonderingly, the Lord Jesus stooped down and kissed the child on the forehead ; and she heard him say in a low voice, as he leaned over her, " No more tears."

Then Violet remembered that she had heard those words somewhere before, and she stirred in her sleep, and stretched out her hand towards the table on which lay her mother's Bible, and the book with the spotted cover. But before she could find them, she awoke with a sudden start and a scream, for, from the fort across the river one of the great cannon had been fired off, and which always shook the town from end to end ; and the window-frames were still rattling, and the Noah's ark animals falling down over the cushions beside her, when she awoke.

" What is that ?" she cried, hastily clutching at the rails of her chair to draw herself up from her pillows. " Evelina, what was that dreadful noise ?"

Either Evelina was not in the room or the noise

had deafened her, for she did not answer Violet's question; and before she could speak again or look round, there was another roar of cannon from the fort, and once more the window-frames rattled and the animals fell pell-mell upon the cushioned window-seat beneath.

"Evelina! Evelina! where art thou? why dost thou not answer?" cried Violet, who, suddenly aroused from a delicious dream of rest and peace, had scarcely yet realized either where she was or what was going on.

She sat up now, and gazed around the room with a flushed face and anxious eyes; but no Evelina was there, though the carriage was still drawn out in the middle of the room, and the new brown hat was lying on the coverlet; and gradually Violet remembered that this was the afternoon that she was to have tea with the policeman and Ella under the trees on the hill.

But surely the afternoon must be almost over now, for the evening shadows were already creeping into the room; and the pigeons were clustering on the window-sill beside her, looking for their usual meal, as they always did ere they went to roost.

"Evelina, where art thou?" she cried once more, as she gazed at the door leading into the little room which once had been her mother's long ago; but no answer came from there either, only another dreadful roar from the cannon, which put all the pigeons to flight, and pitched Noah's wife headlong on the carpet.

Violet had often heard them firing from the fort before, so, after the first three or four great bangs, it did not frighten her so much, only it made her head ache; but presently, leaning a little forward and looking through the window opposite her chair, she saw now that some great event must have happened, for people were racing down the street eagerly, and some were waving their hats, and some had on no hats at all, while, far off in the distance, she could hear a great sound of voices like a deafening cheer of joy.

Again the cannon roared, and again there came the same hoarse shout, which seemed to come from somewhere down near the barracks. And now the people in the street were shouting also as they ran along; and so eager and breathless was their race, that when a woman stumbled and fell on the pathway no one turned to lift her up, or to notice the white face which for many minutes afterwards remained turned up motionless towards the sky.

At last another woman, dressed in black, came out of a shop opposite, with a cup of water in her hand: she waited until the street was pretty clear, and then, crossing over, she put the cup to the woman's lips and helped to raise her up.

Violet could hear the woman's voice speaking comfortingly to her companion, for the narrow casement which formed part of the great window looking over the street was open, and through it a soft breeze was coming in, which blew straight from the hill; and by-and-by, when the woman who had fainted was able to walk, she saw the other lead her across the street, and she distinctly heard her say, " Ah, is not this good news for the town?   Now in Edelsheim we shall have no more tears."

" No more tears!"   They were the same words that Violet had just heard in her dream.   She listened eagerly if she could hear more; but the woman had evidently gone into the little toy-shop close by, and another roar from the cannon set her trembling again, and her heart beat wildly against her little purple frock as she heard again—and this time nearer than before—a deafening shout of men and women's voices rising high upon the evening air.

" Evelina! Evelina!" she cried, striving with trembling lips to make her voice heard above the din and uproar, " come, come to Violet.   Will no one come to Violet?"

But it was quite useless to call or cry out " Evelina." The girl had evidently gone out, and though tears of fear and disappointment streamed from Violet's eyes, and poured down over her little flushed cheeks, no one came to wipe them away or to comfort her.

The cannon, too, roared louder and faster than ever; and all at once the great church bell at the foot of the street began to ring, and clanged out great strokes which set the whole air trembling, so that Violet thought even the blue sky over the house-tops was shaking with the din.

But soon this blue sky began to change to a pale green, and then golden streaks came across it; and presently again broad bands of red, and all the green hill seemed on fire, till at last the great red sun dropped down behind it, and a gray light stole over all; and still Violet sat all alone in the window, while every church bell in the town was jangling, and the roar of voices came up hoarsely from the public gardens down by the barracks.

She could not see across the street to the Adlers' house, for the blind which Evelina had drawn down beside her chair hid their windows from her sight, and there was no one stirring outside who could hear her cry, for the rush of the people towards the market-place was over, and the street had become utterly silent and deserted.

As the darkness crept on, a dreadful fear came over the child's mind that she was going to be left alone in the room all the night—that Evelina had perhaps gone back to Gützberg, or that some accident had happened to her in the street.

The corners of the room were growing dusky, and there were sounds of mice nibbling in the cupboard beside her. The bells in the town ceased ringing, and a dreadful silence seemed to fall over everything. Presently one of the mice stole out of the cupboard, and passing close to the foot of Violet's chair, climbed up the cord of the canary bird's cage, and squeezing itself in through the bars, disappeared in a twinkling.

Even the lantern man had forgotten to come and light the lamp outside her window; and the pigeons had reluctantly deserted their posts on the sill outside, and retired to roost without their evening meal.

"If only I could get out of this chair; if only I could walk; if only some one would come and open the door." And poor Violet moved restlessly to and fro in her chair, and craned her neck to see beyond the strip of narrow blind which hid the opposite house from her view.

The window which looked across to the hill lay wide open, and every now and then a breeze came rushing in, which blew her hair softly about her face and refreshed her; but the hill itself lay now like a great black heap against the evening sky. No friendly moon was up, to frost the branches of the distant trees with silvery light, and only a few faint stars twinkled now and again through the gathering darkness.

Presently she grew quite desperate, and strove in the foolishness of her fear to free herself from the bands which held her fast in her chair. She clutched at the blind, and tried to drag it down; and she called aloud frantically to Madam Adler, to Evelina, to Ella, to any one, to come and help her. But no one answered her, and she sank back, tired out, on the pillows behind her.

Then some one in a neighbouring house began to sing, and she felt comforted. The first note of a human voice, which sounded not so far off, gave her some confidence, and she dragged herself up painfully and listened.

It was a song which she had heard before, but at first she could not remember the words. The air was intensely sad, for Evelina had sung it one night when Violet was lying awake in her bed, and she remembered that she had put her fingers in her ears that she might not hear the words; but now, with a strange eagerness, she leaned forward.

The woman was singing with all her heart. She

scarcely touched the notes of the old piano on which she was accompanying herself; and by-and-by the words came out with a cruel clearness upon the evening air.

Violet knew now who it was. It was the woman who kept the little toy-shop a few doors off, and whose husband, Ella told her, had been killed in the war.

She had a little spinet, not very musical, on which Violet had often heard her play in the pleasant spring evenings before the war began; but, until this evening, the spinet had been silent for many a long day, and the woman's voice had been silent too. To-night it seemed as if she must cry out to some one,—

"My love is dead, and I am left alone."

Violet listened so earnestly to the words, she was so anxious not to lose one of them, that for a time she forgot her own sorrows, and only thought of the poor woman who was never to see her husband any more, and whose heart seemed so terribly sad in that house only a few doors off.

But presently the mouse plumped down out of the cage overhead almost upon her very knees, and startled her so that she screamed aloud; indeed she screamed several times, and clutched once more at the window-blind to try and drag it aside. And then she paused, for she fancied she had heard a step in the street beneath; and by-and-by she was sure there was a footstep slowly and stealthily creeping up the stairs towards the door of her room.

But no one knocked or asked permission to enter; only there was a slight rustling against the wood, as if some one were waiting and listening outside.

Violet, whose heart had leaped up with joy at the first sound of a human step, now felt terrified. A sudden sickness came over her; the wind from the hill blew in chilly through the window, and seemed to pass over her forehead in waves of ice. Her hands grew damp and cold; and the voice outside, singing in its pain "so quite alone," appeared to her to come from miles away and in a kind of curious dream. She fancied that it was the little girl in the book with the spotted cover who was sitting in a window somewhere "so quite alone," and crying out to the Lord Jesus across the roofs and the distant steeple.

But in a moment, and before she had time to reason out this thought or to wonder whether she was awake or dreaming, there was a crash—a loud crackling as if all the houses in Edelsheim were falling to pieces; and as Violet, completely startled out of her faintness, sat up and looked out of the window, it appeared to

her that the gray clouds over the hill had suddenly
split open, and that hundreds of fairy snakes were
rushing up with a swift fury through the sky. This
was immediately succeeded by the same loud sound of
voices which she had heard so often through the evening; and then in a moment the fairy snakes were
gone, and the sky was full of pale red and green stars
falling softly in a shower of beauty to the earth.

"Evelina!" she cried once more, in a piteous entreaty, full of the agony of fear, "Evelina! where art
thou?"

There was a knock at the door now; and Violet,
forgetful, in her new terror, of the step she had heard
a moment ago on the stairs, cried out eagerly, "Come
in."

The door opened. Her eyes were still full of the
red and green stars which she had seen falling outside
over the dark outline of the hill, so for a moment
she was dazzled, and could not see who had entered;
but all at once, as the figure drew quite close to her
chair, she called out loudly and lovingly, "My friend!
my friend!" and threw her arms round the neck of
the old policeman.

"Ah, thou art frightened, little maiden," he said
softly; "and quite alone," he added, looking keenly
around the room as he knelt down beside her chair

and took the two icy hands in his. The action and the tenderness of the touch brought back for a moment the thought of her father.

"Yes, oh so frightened," she said, "and so lonely;" and she laid her head wearily against the shoulder of her protector. "It was so good of thee to come." Then suddenly she turned her face inwards against his cloak, for once again there came that fearful crackling noise down by the hill, and hundreds of fiery snakes again rushed upwards athwart the dark gray sky.

"There, there! little darling, sweetest child! thou must not be so afraid; there is nothing to frighten one, only splendid fireworks which the people in the town are sending up to show their joy."

"Fireworks! and are they only fireworks?" gasped Violet, still keeping her face pressed in close to the old man's heart; "and thou art sure that they are only fireworks?"

"Yes; look out now and see how lovely they are. Blue and yellow and red stars are falling to the ground."

"I do not like to look, it makes my heart go so fast."

There was no need to tell him that fact, for the little fluttering heart was beating at that moment with terrifying speed against his bosom; so he rose up

and drew down the blind across the window, and then
he returned quietly to the chair and placed his arm
tenderly around the little trembling figure.

"And hast thou been long alone, poor little maiden?"
he asked softly, as he lifted the damp hair off her
forehead and stroked her cheek.

"Yes, a long time," she sighed.

"Where is thy maid?"

"I do not know. I awoke, and she was not here.
It was quite bright daylight—oh, such long hours ago.
And I was to go in the carriage father made for me
to the hill, and Ella too, and—" Violet paused and
hesitated, and a burning blush covered all her face.
She had remembered suddenly about the tea under
the trees on the hill, and that the old policeman was
to have been there too.

"Well," he said curiously, as she paused and
hesitated.

"Then I awoke, and all the people were running
screaming down the street, and the bells made such
a noise, and I was frightened."

"And no one was here to tell the good news?"

"What good news?"

"Ah, now I have something to gladden thy poor
little heart with—great news. There has been a
great victory for us. The war, people think, is over;

and soon all our loved ones may come home to us again."

" My father?" cried Violet, sitting suddenly upright in her chair and gazing into the policeman's face with eyes which, even in the gloom of the shaded room, shone with a more wonderful light than the violet stars which were falling again in a shower of beauty on the hill outside.

" Yes, thy father, dearest maiden ; he will soon be home : and that is why the people ran so fast in the street this afternoon, and why they are so noisy now, sending up rockets and making such a riot, screaming and shouting."

" How soon ? " asked Violet in a scarcely audible voice, for the sick faintness she had felt before was returning.

" Ah, that I have not heard ; but if all be true it cannot be very long—a month or so at most."

Violet sighed unconsciously. " I am so—so tired," she said, almost under her breath.

" Poor little maiden ! it is weary work waiting."

" When the lambs are very tired, and cannot walk any more, the Lord Jesus lifts them in his arms and carries them, does he not ? " she said dreamily.

" Yes, yes, of course."

" And dost thou know, my friend, that I saw that

lamb's face, and it was Violet's; and the Lord Jesus was going to put her into her mother's arms to rest herself."

"When? where?" asked the policeman, growing frightened at the words which the child was so slowly uttering; and even in the darkness he could see the strange paleness of the little face.

"In the meadow with the other little girl."

"What little girl?"

"The little one who sent me this watch. She was a very sick little girl like me—oh, so sick the doctor said; but she flew up in the spring with the flowers and the larks to heaven, and she—"

At this moment a loud clattering on the stairs outside made itself heard over everything, and the door of the room burst open with a startling haste.

It was Ella, breathless and panting loudly, who, rushing blindly forward in the darkness, first fell over the handle of the carriage which stood in the middle of the room ready for its first journey, and then over a low stool by the stove. She recovered herself quickly, however, and made for the corner where the dim outline of Violet's head was visible against the holland blind.

"Violet, hast thou heard the news? Evelina has stopped to buy thee a cake at the shop, so I ran on

ever so fast to tell it to thee first. There is a great
battle which is all over, and we have a great victory
and lots and lots of people killed, and a whole town
tumbled down, and the man with the big nose, the
grand emperor we saw in the picture, is all beaten
into little pieces, and had to give up his sword to our
king, and he will soon be put in prison; is not that
splendid? And they sent up fire into the sky and
frightened Ella, and lots of it tumbled down again,
and stars and blue things; and a great red-hot stick,
fell on the shoulders of the orange-girl and made her
give such a hop and a scream. And—and—who is
that sitting in the window beside thee?" Ella
paused, her breath almost gone, and not a little
frightened at the strange figure sitting wrapped in a
cloak beside Violet's chair.

"Will Evelina soon be here?" asked Violet plaintively; for the noise and the fuss were overpowering
her.

"Yes; Evelina is here," replied a voice at the door.
"Ah, poor little maiden! all in the dark. But it is
not my fault, as I will explain to thee. See, here is a
lovely cake I have bought for thy supper. Thou
wert so fast asleep I just slipped down a moment to
hear the grand news, and then the crowd was so
great one could not budge a foot. I thought a

hundred times of thee and thy carriage, but we could never have dragged thee a foot through the throngs of people: and besides, that faithless old policeman never turned up, and I suppose forgot all about thee; but I will make him answer for it to-morrow," she added with a light laugh.

"The policeman is here to answer for himself," said a voice coming out of the darkness; and between Evelina and the window there rose up a figure tall and dark, and to her eyes terrible to look at.

"Oh! who is that?" she cried hastily.

But no one replied to her question; only the figure in the window bent down low over the chair on which Violet sat, and said softly in her ear,—

"Dearest little maiden, the old policeman was not faithless; he did not forget thee, but he was sent for by his captain, and had to go to the gardens to keep order. Please God, to-morrow I will take thee to the hill. And now thou wilt say 'Good-night,' wilt thou not? and go to bed and rest, and dream of the good news of the home-coming, and the good father's joy to see his Violet once more. Good-night, little heart's love."

Violet stretched up her arms and drew the kind grave face down to her.

"Good-night, my friend," she said lovingly.

"Ah, now I can hear thy watch ticking," he said in a hoarse whisper, "and it seems to say something to me."

"What does it say?"

"It says, 'Forget me not.'"

"What?" said Violet, clutching eagerly at his coat; but he had stood up now and was fixing his helmet firmly on his head. Evelina, abashed and confounded, had moved noiselessly into the inner room, and Ella was gaping with open mouth at Violet's friend.

"Good-night," he said once more, in a hoarse voice; "and to-morrow, if all be well, we shall have tea under the trees on the hill."

"Yes, yes, yes," cried Ella joyfully, and forgetting her shyness she flung her fat arms around the knees of the advancing policeman; "and Ella may come too, may she not?"

"Certainly; Miss Ella must come also. And now thou wilt take my hand, and I will leave thee at thy mother's house, for the little maiden in the chair is very tired, and she must sleep and rest.—Good-night," he cried once more as he reached the door and looked back.

"Good-night," she replied with eagerness; and then in a low voice he heard her say softly, "Forget me not."

CHAPTER XXI.

A GUILTY CONSCIENCE.

THE next morning rose beautiful and bright and fair. The town was gay as gay could be; flags were hung from almost every window, and the hum of a great content seemed to fill the air.

In Violet's room all was still. The carriage had been pushed back into the corner of the room, and the little girl was asleep. She had been sleeping nearly all the morning; indeed so profound was her repose that Evelina had grown nervous and summoned the doctor, whose carriage she had seen outside the toy-shop door.

He came in quietly and stood beside the bed. The child's breathing was quick and regular, and her hand lay softly open upon the counterpane. "How long has she slept like this?" he asked in a low voice of Evelina, who stood with tearful eyes near the window.

"Ever since last night when I put her to bed. It

was the news of the victory, sir, which I think upset her."

" Who told her of it ?"

" Little Ella, sir, Madam Adler's daughter."

" Ah, of course, of course, children will talk ; and she must have heard it some time or other. Has she spoken at all since morning ?'

" A few words, sir, but not much sense in them ; about larks and flowers, and about wings—she is always rambling on to me about having wings."

" She will soon have them," said the doctor shortly.

" What !" said Violet, opening her eyes suddenly and looking up; " is that true ? will Violet soon have wings ?"

" Yes, my poor little child, very soon."

" Oh, how beautiful ! how lovely !" she said with a sigh of the utmost content. Then turning her head suddenly, she said quickly, " Fritz, dost thou hear what the doctor says ? Violet will soon have wings." Then she closed her eyes again and fell asleep.

" We can do nothing for her," said the doctor, as he moved aside from the bed. " This stupor that she has fallen into is the result of the shock she received yesterday; for in her state good news is almost as disturbing in its results as bad. I think she may awake out of this sleep and be perhaps none the worse, but we cannot tell. God is very merciful, and the thread of her life is in his hands."

" Yes, sir," said Evelina faintly.

" Has she spoken at all to-day of her father ?"

" No, sir, not exactly; only once she said something about a great victory, and smiled a little."

The doctor turned back and looked again at the quiet face on the pillow, and repeated in a low voice several times the words, " A great victory." " Yes, poor Violet ! thy victory too is close at hand; and then cometh the peace which passeth all understanding."

" I shall come again to-night," he said, as he turned away towards the door; " and meanwhile no one must enter this room to disturb her, nor must she be left alone for a moment. Remember, she has been intrusted to your care by her father, and to mine, and we are responsible for her."

" Yes, sir; I shall watch her very carefully," replied Evelina humbly.

When the doctor was gone, Evelina sat down on the chair by the stove and cried bitterly, for a miserable feeling of guilt was over her. The smile on Violet's face was more difficult for her to look at now than the wakeful restlessness of pain and weariness; indeed everything in the room seemed to reproach her this morning : the carriage standing in the corner; the little brown hat with its wreath of buttercups, which something in Evelina's heart told her would never be asked for again; the cake, which had not been tasted; the window-sill littered with the fallen animals which had been shaken from their usual resting-place by the firing of the cannon; and a kind of dull consciousness resting over all that the end was close at hand, and that the child lying so quietly on the bed yonder was, oh so near heaven;—and she—where was she? and what did she know of that peace which the doctor said passed all understanding?

She stood up presently, and going over to the bed, opened the dead mother's Bible. Between the leaves lay the picture which Violet loved so much to look at. Evelina's eye fell on the centre plate, where the little girl was represented seated all alone in the garret-room, looking out over the roofs and the chimneys towards the far-off sky.

"All alone," she murmured, reading the print beneath it; then turned on hastily, for it seemed to remind her painfully of her conduct yesterday. Presently she came on the lock of golden hair which Violet prized so highly, the long, glistening curl tied up with a knot of black ribbon, and she lifted it up carefully and looked at it with interest; then walking softly across to a little mirror which hung against the wall, she laid it against her own golden curls, and said under her breath, "Just the same colour." She put back the hair into the Bible; and then some other thought following quickly on the comparison, she went over to the trunk which stood beside Violet's bed, and, lifting the lid noiselessly, drew out once more from the corner the hat trimmed with the blue forget-me-nots, which she carried into her own room and presently closed the door.

Meanwhile Violet, quite unconscious that her most precious possessions were being ruthlessly trifled with in the adjoining chamber, slept on quietly. She did not rouse up until quite late in the afternoon, when she saw Evelina sitting in the window-seat as usual, and knitting stockings for the Gützberg children.

"I am going soon to see father," she said softly; but at the words, Evelina, who was in a reverie, started violently, and almost let the knitting slip from her fingers.

"Aunt Lizzie will be glad when father comes home; will she not, Evelina?"

"Yes, of course; every one will be glad."

"And the children, the little cousins at Gützberg, —will not they too be delighted?"

"Oh, they are too young to know such things."

"But they will be watching all this time for thee to go back."

"So thou art thinking already of sending me back to Gützberg?"

"No, no," cried Violet, blushing hotly; "I do not want to send thee away, only Aunt Lizzie said she could spare thee a little while, and now it is so long since father went; and when he comes home he will take care of me all day long, and never be the least bit tired; and I will tell father how good thou hast been to me all this long time."

"I had a letter from thy aunt this morning," said Evelina, turning away her face towards the window; "only a few lines. She is coming over here in a few days to see thee; and probably if thy father returns I shall go back with her. She sent thee her love, and she is making thee a little cloak to wear when thou goest out in thy carriage."

"Ah, how good. I will wear it when father takes me out; that will not be long to wait."

When the doctor came again in the evening, he was quite delighted with the brightness of the little face, and with the rare happy smile which was lighting up all its features.

Violet chatted to him more naturally than she had done for many a long day. She showed him her carriage; and told him of the cloak Aunt Lizzie was making for her; and laughed when she said how the cannon-shot had thrown down Noah's wife and all the animals."

"I may see Ella to-morrow, may I not?" she asked wistfully, as he moved towards the door.

"Certainly; if she is not too noisy."

"Oh, Ella is always good," she cried joyously; "and I am never lonely when she is here."

Madam Adler, too, came across in the evening. Her heart was full of anger against Evelina for having deserted her charge the day before; but when she entered the room and found Violet sitting on Evelina's knee by the stove, with her arms round the girl's neck, who was singing to her, she thought the reprimand would be ill-timed, and she determined to wait for a better opportunity.

CHAPTER XXII.

A STARTLING MESSAGE.

It was not many days before the town of Edelsheim awoke to the fact that the war was not over, and that though the French emperor was a prisoner, France seemed determined to fight to the bitter end.

The gay flags which had been hung out of the windows so joyfully were now rolled up again and put aside, and the people went about their work with dejected faces, awaiting the dread tidings that their loved ones were ordered to march forward towards Paris, and fight the enemy there.

But Violet knew nothing of all this. Secure in the certainty of her father's speedy return, she sat daily in the window watching. She very seldom spoke now; it seemed to tire her. But she smiled to herself much oftener than she had hitherto done, and waved her little thin hand to Fritz, who was ever on the watch in the house opposite; and constantly, in the warm autumn evenings, when the windows of both houses were open, he called across to her and told her his news.   Violet smiled and nodded her head, but she had no strength to call back again, nor even to draw up the cord of the little basket into which Fritz was constantly dropping little gifts and scraps of paper, on which were printed in large letters messages of love and comfort :—" Fritz will soon be well enough to see Violet "—" Fritz is making a boat for Violet ;" and once or twice, in a very closely-folded message, were the words, " Fritz is always asking God to make Violet well."

But at last there came a message from Fritz which roused her for a time out of her lethargy, and set her heart beating wildly.

It was a beautiful autumn evening ; the town was rosy red in the sunset, and all the casements of the oriel window lay wide open.   Violet, who had not spoken for several hours, was lying back on her pillows half sleeping, half waking, with her eyes dreamily fixed on the hill, which was wrapped in a soft purple mist.   The canary bird was picking out the loose feathers from its wings in the cage overhead ; and the old jackdaw on the opposite side of the street, for a wonder was at rest, with his head tucked under his wing.

Fritz for a long time had been making signals to Violet from the high-up dormer window of the house; but her face had been turned away, and though her eyes were fixed on the far-off hill, she saw nothing but a waving meadow bright with flowers, over whose green fragrant grass she was passing with a delicious freedom, her feet not actually touching the ground, only here and there skimming over the cool meadow grass, while a refreshing air wafted her along without fatigue and without pain.

She often had this fancy now, that she was floating along over the earth, that she was free from the ache in her back and the weary heaviness of her limbs; and this afternoon she was listening again to that voice from the meadow saying, " I am going to lay this poor tired lamb in its mother's bosom."

But all at once, when she was seeking once more to see the face of the child which the Lord Jesus held so lovingly in his arms, the basket-bell rang with a sharp tinkle overhead, and she awoke from her dream to find herself no longer wandering amid green pastures, but propped up among her pillows, oh so tired, and with a sudden tearful longing to lay her head against some loving heart and be at rest.

At the sound of the bell, Evelina, who had been dozing also in a chair near the stove, started up angrily, and going over to the window, looked down into the street.

"Ha! it is just as I thought, thou little donkey. Hast thou no sense, Master Fritz, but to go and ring bells in people's ears when they are asleep? See, now, thou hast startled Violet out of her dreams, and she will be ill all the night."

"No, no," said Violet eagerly; but there were sudden tears of distress and weakness standing in her uplifted eyes.

"Look in the basket, Violet," cried Fritz, taking no notice of Evelina's wrath; "there is something in it that I want thee to see, and it is all—" Before, however, Fritz could finish his sentence, his mother had appeared in the doorway, and seizing Fritz by the collar of his coat, had dragged him backwards into the bakery.

"I will not have thee disturbing Violet with thy folly," she said angrily, and pushed him into the back passage.

Meantime Evelina, her own curiosity aroused, had drawn up the little cord from which dangled the basket.

"It is uncommonly light," she said, as she lifted it in at the window. "It strikes me, if I am not mistaken, that Master Fritz is at his old pranks again.

Yes, it is just as I thought; the basket is quite empty.
It is just a silly trick he has played upon thee, and
nothing else." Evelina turned the basket upside down
as she spoke, and shook out some old dried moss and
withered leaves, and a little scrap of dirty paper
folded into a minute size, which fluttered down and
lit on the window-seat beside Violet.

"Little wretch! I shall box his ears the next
time I see him," cried Evelina angrily. "To come
and waken people up for such a senseless joke."

"There was something in the basket," pleaded
Violet in a low voice.

"I tell thee there was not," replied Evelina sharply;
"unless thou callest a handful of dead leaves something."

The child's eyes rested wistfully on the little scrap
of folded paper lying almost within her reach on the
window-seat, but she said nothing. When Evelina was
vexed, Violet felt afraid of her; and besides, she
was down on her knees now gathering the moss and
dirt off the floor, and she did not like to trouble her
further.

But Evelina's tempers were never of long duration.
When she stood up again she was smiling, and said
with a laugh,—

"I have a mind to go across the street and tie this

basket on to Master Fritz's back and hunt him up and down the town for his pains. At any rate, the next time it happens I shall just cut the cord, and then there will be an end of it all."

"No, no, thou wilt not do that, Evelina," cried Violet, stretching out her hands eagerly.

"There is no saying what Evelina might do when she is angry," replied the girl, laughing lightly as she dropped the basket once more out of the window. "Ah, there is the newsman in the street and lots of people gathered round him; I must run down for a moment and see what fresh telegrams have come in. I shall just buy a paper from him and be back immediately."

Violet nodded her head silently, and Evelina, having again arranged the cord in its place, left the room.

When the door was closed, and Evelina's flying footsteps were distinctly audible in the street beneath, Violet tried to stretch out her hand for the piece of paper which had fluttered down out of the basket on to the window-seat beside her; but she found, to her grief, that it was just an inch or two beyond the reach of her finger-tips. She looked round for something with which she could draw it nearer to her, and at last, after some difficulty, she succeeded with the help of the spotted book in pushing it to the edge of the cushion, where she could stretch out her hand and take hold of it.

Even this little exertion tried her. She panted, and for some moments did not attempt to open the paper. Her heart beat quickly and her hands trembled. She did not believe that Fritz had been playing a trick upon her, and she guessed that there was some special piece of news to be found in the little crumpled scrap which she held tightly pressed up in her hand.

At last she opened it out, and as she read the words printed across it in large letters she gave quite a sharp cry and started up in her chair.

"Ella is going to be an angel, and have wings."

This was the whole message—no explanation, no other word to give a hint or a reason, and no Fritz at the window opposite to make things clear.

She stared again at the words. Her cheeks grew crimson, her eyes darkened, tears came into them and fell upon the dirty scrap of paper on her knee.

Ella was going to have wings! Ella, who could run and jump and walk and was never tired; who could laugh and sing and hop and follow Fritz wherever he went. Ella was going to have wings!

And Ella had no hump upon her back, no pain, no tiredness. She had not been waiting for them long, oh, so long as she had! A great lump came struggling up into her throat, drops of sweat gathered on her forehead. The book with the spotted cover lay across her knees; the tears came splash, splash upon the yellow binding; and Violet, bending her head down lower, said in a sobbing whisper,—

"Oh, dear Lord Jesus! canst thou not also give wings to Violet? Violet is so tired, and cannot walk or run." Then followed another long sob and a shower of burning tears, in the midst of which the door opened and Evelina came laughing in, her eyes brimming with fun and her whole manner joyous and gay.

"Did any one ever hear of such an idea?" she cried, flinging herself down on a chair. "To make that great fat Miss Ella an angel! the very thought of it gives one almost a fit. I could almost die of laughter.—But what is the matter with the child? What art thou crying for, Violet?" and Evelina rose and came over to Violet, whose head was bent upon her purple frock, and her face was covered with her hands.

"What troubles thee? Look up, Violet, and hear my news. There is going to be a great procession through the town. The general is coming home wounded from the war. Such a brave old fellow!

he has had both his arms shot off, and two of his
sons have been killed in the battle of Sedan; so all
Edelsheim is going out to meet him on his return and
give him a welcome. And there are to be hundreds of
girls dressed in white, who are to sing beautiful songs
and scatter flowers on the road; and a whole band of
little angels, who are to have wings, and they are to
sing too. And just imagine—Ella over the way is to
be an angel! Such an idea! one might just as well
make an angel of a little fat, squeaking pig; but
of course it is for her voice they want her. Ah,
Miss Violet, it is a shame for thee to go on crying
so when I have brought thee home such a grand
piece of news. What ails thee? Look up and tell
me."

"I want to be an angel too," cried Violet with a
bursting sob.

"An angel! Ah, is that it? Poor little darling!
thou wilt be an angel soon enough."

"But Ella will have wings first, and will fly away
from Violet, and Violet is so lonely."

"Miss Ella fly!" cried Evelina, throwing up her
hands again and bursting into a fresh fit of laughter.
"Why, it would take all the wings in the town to
lift her off her feet. No, no; do not be afraid; Miss
Ella will not fly."

"Could not I go with the other little angels?" sobbed Violet.

"Ah, no, no, my treasure; that would be impossible. Thou canst not walk, and it is a long way to the station."

"But if I had wings."

"Yes, yes, of course, if thou hadst wings that would be another thing; then thou couldst fly wherever thou hadst a wish," said Evelina soothingly, for the pleading eyes so full of their sorrow pained her.

"And the doctor said, soon, very soon, Violet would have them; and perhaps God would give Violet wings that very day, and then she could go with all the other angels. Is it not so, Evelina?"

"Yes, yes; of course, when the Lord Jesus gives Violet wings then she can go where she likes."

"I will ask him, yes, I will ask him," said Violet softly; and through her tears there broke a sweet struggling smile as she lifted her eyes to the sky above the shadowy hill and held communion with her God.

CHAPTER XXIII.

GREAT PREPARATIONS.

THE morning of the procession had come—such a glorious morning!—bright sunshine, blue sky, and a soft breeze blowing down from the hill. At an early hour the whole town was astir. Every one was anxious to join in or to see this procession; for the brave general for whose home-coming it was planned was the favourite of the town, and all were anxious to do him honour.

It seemed to them only a few days ago that they had seen his sturdy figure walking down the shady alley accompanied by his sons, fine fair-haired young fellows, who had since then fallen wounded to death in the dreadful battle of Sedan.

Those whose work could be got over in the early morning rose with the sun, so as to leave the afternoon free to do honour to their general. The washer-women at the river's edge were battering their linen on the stones from early dawn, while the usually

sulky river crept in to-day bright with little rivulets
of gold; and the walls of the gray old castle were
gay with flags, whose shining spear-heads caught the
first rays of the rising sun.

In the streets the pigeons were already pecking
happily, for the noisy tread of the early risers had
disturbed them; and beneath the windows of Violet's
house a whole cluster were collected, Madam Adler
having already risen and thrown out to them a large
sieveful of corn which she had brought from the
bakery for the purpose.

She looked up at Violet's window before she turned
to re-enter the shop, and sighed heavily. She had
been, in the evening before, to see her little darling,
and to show her Ella dressed in her angel's garments,
—soft white raiment, and glistening wings. But the
effect on Violet had been so overpowering that
Madam Adler had hurried Ella away, and had herself been obliged to listen to a lecture from Evelina
for having so thoughtlessly broken in on the child's
evening sleep and set her heart beating with a distress
too deep for words.

Madam Adler had made no reply to Evelina's
reproaches, for her own heart was too full of pain, to
see the great change which had lately come over the
little wan face; and when she saw the sudden lustre

which burned in Violet's eyes at the first sight of
Ella with the white dress and the shining wings, and
then listened to the passionate sobbing which followed, she had gone back to her own house over-
whelmed with grief at the result of her visit, and she
longed for the day of the procession to be over, that
the subject might pass away from Violet's mind, and
Ella's wings be folded up and put away.

Ella, upstairs in her room, was awake also this
morning at an unusually early hour. She could not
rest, with the joyous expectation of being an angel
and walking in the great procession; and ever so
many times she had risen and gone over and touched
with her soft, fat fingers the wings so beautifully
tipped with silver and shining with stars, and which
lay upon the table in the middle of the room: but
every time she looked at them a sorrowful remembrance
came over her of Violet's face and her bitter tears;
and at last the little girl walked back to her bedside,
and kneeling down said softly,—

"Oh, thou good Lord Jesus, be very kind to poor
Violet in the house opposite, and give her wings too,
like Ella!"

She looked up very steadily at the ceiling as she
said these words. Her wide-open eyes seemed to
see far up above the roof and the chimneys and the

storks. The soft yellow hair was straggling out in long loops and curls from under her linen night-cap, her elbows rested on the bed, and her dimpled fingers were clasped. Was she, after all, so unlike an angel, this "fat Miss Ella," at whose appearance Evelina could not restrain her laughter?

When Ella had finished her little prayer, and was just saying "Amen" in a rather loud voice, the door opened and Fritz walked in.

"What art thou doing, Ella?" he said rather curiously. "Out of bed already, at this early hour, and saying thy prayers! Dost thou think thou art an angel already?"

Ella blushed crimson as she stood up, and she shuffled her little pink feet over each other uneasily on the carpet.

"It was only about Violet," she said nervously, and her eyes travelled back again to the wings shining so softly on the dark oil-cloth cover of the table.

"So thou hast been thinking of her too," said Fritz, drawing a deep breath. "I have thought of nothing else all night, and that is why I too am up so early, and dressed, as thou seest, for going out."

Ella had noticed that Fritz had his cap in his hand, and she had wondered at it.

" Well, well ? " she asked open-mouthed.

" Well, I am going off to the police barrack to try and see Violet's friend. Mother told me last night that she heard the procession was not to pass through our street at all, but was to turn up by the cathedral and across the market square to the station ; and then poor Violet could not see it at all, or hear any of the music. Mother says she is glad, but I am not a bit ; for look at this, Ella." Fritz drew from his trowsers pocket a little crumpled scrap of paper and spread it out upon the palm of his hand. " She dropped this out of the window to me last night ;—and I know this one thing." Fritz spoke in a curious, husky voice, and turned away his face.

" What thing, Fritz ? "

" Violet will never send me any more notes. Look at this ;—I was half an hour before I could make it out."

There was a large V, and then a lot of trembling up-and-down strokes without any pretence at printing, only there was a dot over one stroke, and a letter something like a " t " at the end ; then came the word " wants," pretty fairly readable ; then another trembling set of meaningless lines, and the word " angels ; " and again a word which Fritz after much trouble had made out to be " sing."

"Violet wants to hear the angels sing;" that was her message.

"And I am going straight now to the barracks, and I shall show this to our policeman, and he shall go to the general's wife, and they shall arrange together that the procession *is* to go through this street. I have settled it all in the night when I was lying awake."

"Perhaps the general's wife will not do it."

"Perhaps she will, thou little ass," replied Fritz curtly, as he banged the door after him and went out.

"Ah, if I could give Violet my wings," said Ella softly, as, once more returning to the table, she touched the silver pinions which lay spread out upon it shiningly; "but the good Lord Jesus is much much kinder than Ella, and perhaps he will lend her some wings just for this one day."

Ella went over to the casement and looked across and down at the closed shutters of Violet's window. She was singing softly to herself the words of the angels' song, which her mother had with much care been teaching to her for the last few days,—

> "Angels, sing on, your faithful watches keeping,
> Sing us sweet fragments of the songs above,
> Till morning's joy shall end the night of weeping,
> And life's long shadows break in endless love."

Ella had the sweetest childish voice that one could

hear anywhere : yes, it was for this reason she had been chosen to form one of the angel-choir, and now as she came to the end of her verse, she sang out the chorus loud and clearly,—

" Angels of Jesus,
Angels of light,
Singing to welcome
The pilgrims of night."

Ella did not quite understand what the words of the hymn meant, though her mother had given many long minutes to their explanation. She only knew they were about the good Lord Jesus, and she felt that they were words Violet would love to hear ; so she sang them loud enough and clear enough for the sound to reach her ears were she awake.

But there was no stir in the oriel window except a burst of song from the canary opposite, behind whose cage the curtains of Violet's casement had been loosely folded ; but the blind in the room next to hers was at this moment quickly drawn up, and Ella saw Evelina look out hurriedly into the street, and then withdraw as quickly behind the table. She was up early, too, and dressed already in a pretty white and blue muslin dress, which she was evidently trying on before the looking-glass, for Ella saw her take up some blue bows from the table and pin them on her

dress, arranging them first in one place and then in
another until she was satisfied with their effect.

Ella wondered that Evelina should be so smartly
dressed at so early an hour ; but she wondered still
more when she saw her turn back a moment from the
window and then reappear with a large Leghorn hat
in her hand, covered with some pale blue flowers, and
lined with a pretty light blue satin, the same colour
as the ribbon bows upon her dress.

She turned it backwards and forwards for a few
moments, picking up the blue flowers with her fingers,
just here and there where they stuck too closely to
the straw ; and she bent the broad flap a little to one
side, and pinned it up with much care ; and then she
placed it on her head, smiling a little and moving to
and fro in front of the mirror. All at once she
turned and walked away. Ella saw her hurriedly
snap off the hat and throw it on the bed, and then
move forward as if towards Violet's room. Ella
watched for her to come back ; but at last growing
tired of waiting she lay down on her little bed, and, still
humming the angels' chorus, she fell into a light sleep.

Before, however, she had quite wandered off into the
land of dreams the door of her room opened again,
and Fritz came in with flushed face and excited
manner.

" It is all of no use," he cried, flinging his cap down at the foot of the bed. " I have seen the policeman, and he says it is no good for him to ask."

" And he will not even try ?" asked Ella, opening her sleepy eyes.

" Oh yes, he will try. He has gone off now to see the colonel; but he knows it is all no use." Fritz sat down on the side of Ella's little cot, and suddenly burst out crying.

" I wish I had never told her anything about it," he said sobbing.

" Why, dear Fritz ?" and Ella threw her fat arms round her brother's neck.

" That old cat Evelina told the policeman that since I had told Violet about the angels she has had no sleep and can eat nothing, and that in a few days she will be quite dead."

" Quite dead," echoed Ella mournfully; " and poor Fritz will never see her nor speak to her any more."

" Hush, Ella," cried Fritz, springing up from the bed angrily; " Fritz will see her again. Fritz will speak to Violet again. He will go this instant and ask the Lord Jesus this very day to make her quite well, to take all the sickness away from her; and the Lord Jesus must listen to Fritz this time, for he will go out on the very top of the house and call ever so loud, so loud that he must hear him." And Fritz, his face all quivering with the anguish of the moment, started up and rushed wildly out of the room ; and Ella heard his feet ascending the little wooden ladder that led out among the nasturtiums and the red geraniums on to the red-tiled roof above.

CHAPTER XXIV.

A GRIEVOUS DISAPPOINTMENT.

IT was still quite early when Evelina drew back the curtains in the oriel window and let in the rosy morning light.

A few moments before, Violet had startled her by a cry of joy, so keen and unmistakable that she had hurried from the inner room in her white muslin dress to the child's bedside, only to find her face pressed in against the pillow, around which her arms were tightly pressed.

" What is it ? why didst thou call so ?" she cried curiously as she stooped over the bed.

" O Evelina, the angels were singing to me !" said Violet, lifting up a face still wreathed in the happiest smiles. " Didst thou not hear them, Evelina ? I knew the very words they said. And father, dear father, he was there with them in the meadow beside the hill; and he stretched out his hands to me and cried out so loud, ' To meet again,' that I screamed out with joy."

" Ah, that was indeed a lovely dream," said Evelina, stooping over the bed and kissing the little face still lighted up with the straggling beams of heavenly glory. " Go to sleep, dearest one, and perhaps thou mayest dream of the angels again."

" And dost thou know, Evelina, in that meadow beside the hill, where the flowers grow, my feet never touch the ground—never."

" Hush, little heart! go to sleep," she replied softly.

" And thou, Evelina, wilt thou not be an angel too ? for thou art dressed in white, and thou art so lovely and so kind," said the little voice from among its pillows.

Evelina made no answer ; her cheeks burned with a vivid red, and her heart gave loud throbs as she bent over the child and kissed her again passionately; then she turned and went back into the room. But her eyes were full of tears, and for many minutes afterwards she was restless and miserable, until at length she took off the white dress and laid it aside on the top of her trunk; and the hat with the blue forget-me-nots she hastily covered over with a handkerchief, and hid it away in the press.

' What is the boy doing up there ?" she said suddenly as she looked up at the red tiles of the house

opposite. " Why, he is saying his prayers on the roof !
Was ever anything so funny ?"

When Violet did awake later on, she seemed to have
forgotten all about her dream ; she sighed heavily,
and there were bright red spots on her cheeks. She
watched all Evelina's movements with a kind of dull
curiosity, but for a long time she made no effort to
speak. At last she said, with a weak and somewhat
complaining voice, " Evelina, why art thou making
the room ready so early ? That brush knocks so loudly
against the chairs, and Violet's head is aching."

" I am up early because the whole town is up
early," replied Evelina somewhat shortly; " and a room
cannot be cleaned properly without brushing it."

" And why is the whole town up early—why,
Evelina ?"

" Why ? of course thou knowest that this is the day
of the grand procession, and one cannot be both inside
of the house doing one's work and outside of it at the
same time enjoying oneself."

" And art thou going out to see the angels ?" asked
Violet, fixing her eyes sorrowfully on the face of
Evelina.

" That depends—I am not certain."

" But thou wouldst like it, wouldst thou not ?"

" Yes, yes, of course."

" And will it be a long way off, down a far, far street ?"

" No, no, quite close.   They are to turn off at the fountain and go up by the cathedral."

" Then Violet will perhaps hear them singing," cried the child, raising herself on her elbow, and flushing all over a lovely carmine colour.   " I have often heard the women singing at the fountain in the evening."

" Yes, I daresay."

" Ah, how Violet would love to stand, like other little children in the street, and see the beautiful angels with their wings."   A deep, longing sigh followed this remark.

Evelina made no reply, and Violet still followed her movements wistfully with her eyes, till at last they fell upon the little carriage, which she was at this moment dusting, and which she presently pushed somewhat further back into the corner.

" Just as far as the fountain," pleaded Violet with quivering lips.

" No, no, it is impossible ; for the greatest crowd of all will be just there.   They are all to gather at the fountain, which is to be decked out with flowers ; and the first chorus is to be sung beside it.   To drag a carriage through such a multitude of people would be out of the question."

" But in thine arms, Evelina ; couldst thou not take me such a little way in thine arms ?"

" In my arms, dear love ? who ever heard of such a thing ?"

" Yes, yes, only to the fountain, to see the angels and to hear them sing."

" Thou askest me that which thou knowest well I cannot do," replied Evelina almost angrily. " The doctor would not hear of my taking thee out of thy bed to carry thee in my arms among such a lot of people. And besides, thou wouldst not like it thyself : other children would stare at thee, and say things, perhaps, which would hurt thee."

" What would they say, Evelina ?"

" Ah, cruel things : children do not stop to pick their words."

" But what would they say ?" pleaded Violet, her eyes opening wide and her cheeks flushing.

" They would, perhaps, point their fingers at thee and call thee names. Ah, I have heard such things often in the street. There are wicked children as well as good. I have seen them even throwing stones after little sick children."

" Yes," cried Violet, sitting up straight, and her eyes deepening to the purple shade which always came with some great mental excitement ; " and thou rememberest, Evelina, how one wicked boy threw a great heavy stone at a poor hunchback; and how God was watching, and when they would have thrown another the Lord Jesus laid his hand on the hunchback's shoulders, and out of them came two beautiful shining wings, and he flew straight up to heaven. Thou rememberest all this, Evelina?"

"Oh yes, I daresay," replied Evelina, who was down on her knees polishing the stove.

"But thou didst tell that very story to me."

"Well, and what then?"

"Then Violet is not afraid to go out in the streets; for the good Lord Jesus loves Violet very, very much, and if anything came to hurt her he would just give her wings, and she would fly away straight up to heaven."

For a moment Evelina's heart relented, as she looked up from the stove at those earnest eyes full of such a beseeching entreaty.

"Well, well, we can see when the time comes," she said quickly. "Lie down now, and don't talk about it any more. When I have done my work I will go and see the doctor and ask him; and if he says 'Yes,' why, then, we must arrange it somehow."

"Ah, thou best Evelina, how good thou art!" cried Violet, stretching out her arms gratefully. But Evelina was perhaps too busy to notice the action. At any rate, she continued polishing the stove; and Violet, with eyes still darkly dilated with the wonder of some great but as yet unrealized joy, lay back upon her pillow, only saying to herself in a whisper, "Violet will see the angels and will hear them sing."

At eleven o'clock Evelina went out. She was some time away, and Violet watched with a beating heart for her return. At last she heard footsteps on the stairs; but Evelina, instead of entering the kitchen, went into her own room and shut the door.

Violet waited for a few minutes, and then called to her; but she received no answer. Evelina was walking hurriedly about the inside room, and did not hear her calling.

At last the door opened, and Evelina came in. She had on a white dress now—a white muslin dress, dotted over with pale-blue spots; and on her bosom there was fastened a bunch of forget-me-nots, and on the front of the dress there were also pale-blue bows the same colour as the flowers.

She looked so young and fresh, with her golden hair and her pretty smiling face, covered just now with a crimson blush, that Violet cried out involuntarily,—

"Oh how beautiful! how lovely! Hast thou seen the doctor?"

But Evelina only said hastily, as she looked at the bed, "How stupid of me! I have forgotten to dress the child."

"Then thou *wilt* take me ?   O dearest Evelina, thou art too good to Violet."

Evelina looked now really distressed. She came over and took the child's hot hands in hers, and sat down on the edge of the bed.

"I have not seen the doctor," she said in a quick, nervous voice. "He was out, and had left no word where he was gone. I durst not take thee out on such a day without his leave. Although the sun is hot, there is a keen east wind blowing ; so I will just run down to the fountain and have one look at the procession, and then come back to thee. I shall not be five minutes away, and thou shalt hear all about it when I return, and how Miss Ella looked, and how she sang ; and then we shall have, oh such a feast when Evelina comes home—peaches and grapes which are in the next room waiting for us to eat them, and a cake covered with sugar, and a bunch of violets fastened on the top.   And we shall have such fun ; shall we not, thou little heart's love ?   And now Evelina will dress thee in thy little purple frock; and Miss Ella shall come back, wings and all, and have a share in our supper and our good things.   And now

thou wilt not be an ungrateful little girl, when Evelina has done all this for thee ?   Ah, for shame ! dry
thine eyes, and let us have no more tears."

Violet drew her hand quickly out of Evelina's, and
wiped away the tears which were flowing fast down
her poor pale face; for was it not ungrateful and
unkind of her to weep and fret when Evelina had
been so good, and had bought for her such lovely
things as grapes and peaches ?

Evelina tied an apron over her new dress and began
to comb out Violet's yellow locks.   They did not
glisten now so brightly as they used to do, for long
sickness had dimmed their golden colour; but still,
when tied up with the dark purple knot, they hung
prettily enough over the cashmere dress, into the
neck and sleeves of which Evelina had sewn clean, soft,
white frills.

"There now ! thou art quite lovely, quite charming!"
cried Evelina, gazing at the little girl, whose lips still
quivered with a suppressed excitement.   "And see
here ! I will give thee some of my forget-me-nots, and
thou shalt fasten them, so, on front of thy dress; and
there will not be an angel in all the procession so
fair as thee.   Eh, little heart's darling, what sayest
thou ?"

Violet did not answer; she only lifted her eyes to

Evelina's face, as if she wished to speak and could not.

"What is it? Is there anything more I can do for thee? for it is now on the stroke of twelve, and if I do not start at once I shall be late."

"Please, please, Evelina, take Violet in thine arms, only this once—such a little way to the fountain, such a short, short street—that Violet may see the angels and hear them sing."

"It is impossible," replied Evelina shortly, and growing very red. "But as thou art so determined to cry and to make a fuss, I will stay at home myself, and make an end of it all." And Evelina sat down on a chair, and tears came into her eyes.

"No, no!" cried Violet passionately; "thou must go, Evelina. Violet will cry no more. She will wait here quite quietly till thou comest back. Yes, go now; please go, Evelina, ever so fast; and when thou hast seen the beautiful angels at the fountain, thou wilt come back quickly to Violet."

Evelina rose up with averted face, and said, somewhat sullenly, "Well, as I am dressed, I suppose I may as well go; but after such a fuss and crying one cannot enjoy oneself very much."

She pushed the door of her own room open as she said this, and, going in, drew the bolt quickly across it. A minute or two later she opened the other door at the side of the landing, and began to descend the stairs.

"Evelina!" cried Violet after her piteously, "lift Violet first into the window. Evelina! Evelina! thou hast forgotten to put Violet into her chair!"

Evelina turned to answer the child's appeal; but suddenly remembering something, she paused and raised her hand to her head. "I cannot wait now to take it off, for it is all pinned to my hair," she said peevishly. "In any case, I shall be back directly." And so, turning a deaf ear to Violet's cries, she went down the stairs and out into the street.

CHAPTER XXV.

WINGS AT LAST.

VIOLET waited and listened until the last sound of Evelina's footsteps had died away, and then she fell into a sudden reverie. Her eyes remained fixed on the rails at the foot of her bed, and she neither moved nor spoke—only now and then a little shiver seemed to pass over her, and she sighed heavily, and her eyebrows were contracted with pain.

A sudden sense of great loneliness had come over her, and with it a swift remembrance of her dear mother, the mother who had been carried out through that very door by which Evelina had that moment passed out, and who had never returned to her any more. Ah, had she been here now, she would have listened to her cries; she would have carried her in her arms to the fountain. She would have lifted her up so tenderly, and held her tightly, oh so tightly to her breast; and together they would have listened to the angels singing.

And then again came the recollection of that dream, when the Lord Jesus had met her in the meadow, and had shown her the little lamb which he was carrying in his bosom—the little lamb with the white face, so like Violet. And she remembered the sound of his voice, as he said to her so softly, " See, she has fallen asleep, and I am going to lay her in her mother's arms."

Ah, if Violet could fall asleep like that poor tired lamb, and awake in the arms of her dear mother, whose face she had not seen for so long—oh so long, yes, long, long ago! Again that thrilling shiver passed over her, and the little face grew pale.

" Mother !" she cried—" mother ! canst thou not hear me, mother ? Mother ! mother !" It rose higher and higher now, the wail of a child's despair.

But, hark ! what was that other sound without ? Music—voices—a burst of sudden song somewhere not far off. Violet ceased to cry, and listened with large dilated eyes, from which the pain of the past moment had not yet departed.

" The angels ! the angels ! I hear them singing !" she cried, starting up in an ecstasy of delight. " They are singing at the fountain ; I can hear them. And Ella is with them, and she has wings. Ah, if some one could lift me gently and put me in my chair

at the window !—Kate, Kate, come to Violet; come
quickly."

. She had not long to wait for an answer to her call,
for as she cried aloud for Kate, the old servant pushed
open the door, and walked in. She had not come,
however, at Violet's summons. She held a red-coloured
envelope in her hand, and she looked round the room
anxiously and somewhat angrily.

"So; it is just as I thought. That little conceited
minx has gone out, and left the child all alone. I
just caught a sight of the hat as she whirled by the
window, and I knew well where it came from."

"Kate, Kate, listen to the angels. They are singing at the fountain. If thou speakest so loud, I cannot hear them."

"Ay, ay; I hear them well enough. But who is
to open this telegram and tell us what is in it?"

"Ah, Kate, do not mind what is in it. Lift me in
thy arms, dear Kate, and put me in my chair by the
window."

"Well, have patience a moment, and I will see if
I can make out the words. I am a regular blockhead
at reading; but the messenger is waiting at the door
to see if there is any answer, and that silly girl may
not be back for an hour."

Kate turned a little aside, as she tore open the

envelope, and looked back a moment at Violet with an evident nervousness of manner.

"Ah, God be thanked! it is no bad news. It is from the good lady at Gütsberg. She will be here this afternoon."

But Violet did not hear one word Kate said. A great hope was rising in her bosom. The sound of the angels' voices was drawing nearer and nearer, and she could now almost catch the very words they were singing. It was growing clear to her that the procession must be advancing up the street.

"Kate, Kate, where art thou going?" she cried suddenly, as the old servant moved towards the door. "Wilt thou not carry Violet across to her chair?"

"Yes, yes, in a moment. I am only going to the street door, and I shall be back immediately."

By the time she returned to the room Violet's cheeks were burning with excitement, and there was a look in her eyes which almost frightened the old servant.

"Lift me to the window!" she cried, almost passionately. "The angels are coming! they have wings! I must see them! they are coming up the street!"

Kate held out her arms quickly to the child; but her heart sank as she noticed the crimson cheeks, and the eyes which looked at her and yet did not seem to see her, so full were they of some deep and over-powering excitement.

"Quick, quick! they are in the street!" she repeated feverishly.

"Ay, ay, they are in the street, that is true enough; but have patience, dear heart. There is time enough yet. They are not so near as thou thinkest."

Still Violet repeated the same words furiously—"Quick, quick! they are in the street! they are in the street!"—until Kate had taken her in her arms and carried her into the window.

"Do not put me in the chair; put me on the seat in the middle of the window," she cried eagerly, as Kate would have deposited her in her usual place. "Violet can see so much better all up and down the street, and thou canst put thy arms round me, and hold me so tightly;—is it not so, Kate?" She turned round quickly, and put her burning lips against the old woman's cheek: "The good Lord Jesus holds the sick lambs ever so closely in his arms; and I am one of his lambs, for I saw its face—oh so white!—and it was Violet's."

"Dear heart, she is crazed!" muttered Kate to herself.—"There now; sit down on the seat, and I will hold thee tightly, I warrant."

"The angels! I see them! they are dressed in white!

They are coming nearer and nearer ! Kate, canst thou not see them too ? "

Violet clutched at the wooden box full of sweet violets, which stood on the window-sill outside, and drew herself forward with a sudden access of strength. The box, which was bound by many a cobweb to the mullioned stone, moved one inch or so, and rocked ominously. Two white pigeons, which were preening their feathers on the ledge just beside it, flew away frightened, and perched on the roof opposite.

" Kate, Kate, I see Ella ! She is waving her hand to me; there is a crown in it. Dost thou not see ?— a crown of gold. She is holding it out to me."

" Ay, ay; I see Miss Ella. How fat she looks; and cold too, poor child ! her arms look quite blue in her thin white dress."

" Ah, she looks beautiful—the angels of God are all beautiful. They fly about in heaven and have no pain, Kate. And look at Ella's wings how they shine. Stand up straight, Kate, and thou wilt see better."

Kate leaned a little forward over the child's head and looked out. " Yes, yes; one would almost think that they were real. But here is another messenger coming to the door with a telegram, and there is no one downstairs to take it from him."

"Thou canst go down," cried Violet eagerly. "I am quite safe here in the window, and quite, quite comfortable."

"Thou art sure, dear heart?"

"Yes; I can hold on by the box until thou comest back."

Here all at once the children's voices burst forth in the street beneath, and in a delicious harmony took up the melodious hymn,—

> " Angels of Jesus,
> Angels of light,
> Singing to welcome
> The pilgrims of night."

Ella's clear treble rose up high, high into the air, and seemed to enter in at the very window.

Violet, clutching unconsciously at the box in front of her, drew herself more forward, till at length she was leaning over the sweet-scented leaves, and could see well down into the street beneath.

There was a hush now among the crowd, for all the people gathered in the space below, listening entranced to the sweet childish treble as it rose higher and higher in its anxiety that the song should reach the ear of one the child loved. But all at once the song ceased, and a cry came from her parted lips— "See, see! look up! Violet is at the window, and she will fall."

The white-robed procession paused for a moment at the shrill scream of the child, and all heads were turned up to see what was the cause of her anguish, while at the same moment a woman's voice, uplifted in sudden terror, cried passionately from amongst them, "Violet! ah, wicked child; go back. What art thou doing?"

But Violet did not see the upturned faces, nor hear Evelina's cry of terror-struck reproach. She was alike unconscious of rebuke or fear, for in the street beneath her were gathered a glorious company of angels. Their raiment, white and glistening, dazzled her aching eyes; their crowns of gold seemed all on fire; while the voices of a great multitude rang in her ears in sweet, melodious invitation,—

> " Come, weary soul;
> Jesus bids thee come."

To Violet it was no longer the hot and dusty streets of Edelsheim on which she gazed. She did not see the rocking crowd or the terror imprinted now on every upturned face. No; those who caught a glimpse of her at this moment knew that she saw none of them—that some heavenly vision held her inthralled and amazed. Her lips were white; her eyes burned; she spoke, yet no one heard, till all at once she stretched out her arms with a cry of surpassing ecstasy, and exclaimed, "Mother, dear mother, see! look up! here is Violet."

Then all the people knew what was coming, for the child as she uttered the last words had fallen forward upon the box. It was hopeless to think that Evelina with all her efforts could reach the room in time. The wooden box had turned over on its side, and the loosened clay and the fragrant flowers rattling over their heads and faces gave them timely warning to retreat.

The crowd surged to each side; the angels, who had ceased their singing, recoiled with a terrified rapidity to the farther side of the street. Only one person, with a courageous presence of mind and a fearless love, rushed from amongst them to stay the terrible catastrophe.

But was it, after all, so terrible that the women should faint, and the angels hide their faces in their hands? Only a flutter of a purple frock, a glimpse of golden hair, preceded by a sudden crash as the box of violets fell splintered on the pavement beneath. Then all looked upwards with a scream. But Violet was in the arms of the old policeman, and the shining yellow locks were hanging loosely over his shoulder.

A crowd gathered round him quickly, and the people pressed upon him, while some of the little angels in their silver shoes stood on tiptoe that they might, perchance, catch one glimpse of that white, white face.

Yes, it was white and still, and sad enough to look upon.

"Keep back," cried the policeman sternly, "and let the child have room to breathe."

"She will never breathe again," said the voice of a woman by his side; "the child is stone dead; we can see that for ourselves." It was Madam Adler who spoke, and she held Fritz by the hand, whose face was gray and rigid with fear and horror.

"Keep back, I say; she is not dead. For pity's sake let the child have air!"

There was a slight retrograde movement and then a general start of wonder. Violet had opened her eyes!

For a second, hope rose in every breast; for a smile glimmered and flickered over the poor pale face, and the lips moved. She lifted the drooping arm which had hung so listlessly by her side, and laid it for a moment upon the faithful breast of the old policeman. "My friend," she said softly, and looked up into his eyes with a gaze which was terrible in its steadfastness of love; then the eyelids closed quietly again, and the smile died out.

A hush fell on all the people. Surely this was death.

But there was still a breath, and the little purple frock heaved slowly, and the frill of the white pinafore quivered with a thrilling motion.

All at once she moved, turned her head quickly towards the street, and strove to raise herself in the arms of her friend.

"Fritz, Fritz!" she cried eagerly, in a strange uplifted voice full of a strong appeal.

"Yes, here is Fritz; what is it, dear Violet?"

"Fritz is here," he replied faintly, lifting up an ashen face towards hers.

But Violet's eyes were wide open now, and full of a wonderful joy. They travelled straight up over the housetops and the golden crown of the hill towards the bright blue sky, as if following some vision of delight.

"Fritz!"—it was now a cry of triumph—"it is all quite true. See! look up yonder, high, high up. Ah, seest thou not now Violet has wings?"

All the people with a common consent looked upward as she spoke; but there was nothing there to see but God's blue heaven and a speck of golden cloud sailing slowly past across the mountain top.

When they turned back again they knew then that

the child was dead; for the eyes, full still of that strange purple wonder, were immovably fixed upon the far off heavens, and the awe and majesty of death were creeping into them as the light of life died out.

"Free at last," said the policeman, lifting up his face with a strange grim smile towards the distant sky. "She has escaped like a bird from its cage, and is gone up yonder."

There was nothing more to wait for now. The policeman turned towards the door of Violet's house and carried her away from their eyes. The procession, re-forming, moved mournfully onwards. Some women in the street snatched up bunches of the violets which lay scattered about over the road, and thrust them into their bosoms.

But Madam Adler, Fritz, and little Ella in her silver shoes and shining wings, remained behind, and they and many others followed the old policeman and his burden up the stairs; and Madam Adler, pushing her way on in front, opened the door of the kitchen to allow him to pass in. But there on the threshold they were met by Kate, behind whom stood the form of Evelina rigid with horror and dismay.

"Is it all over ?" cried the old woman distractedly— "is the child dead ?—tell me now at once, is our Violet dead ?"

"Yes, quite dead."

"Thou art certain?"

"Yes, quite certain."

"Then God be praised for all his mercies. She will never know this new trouble which has fallen upon us. Her father is gone also." She held out her hand vaguely towards them all with an open telegraph form crumpled up in her fingers. Madam Adler snatched it from her and read the words, "John was killed this morning in repulsing with his company a sortie of the enemy from the town of Metz."

CHAPTER XXVI.

"NO MORE TEARS."

No more tears for little Violet. Yes, that was the joy which almost stilled their sorrow. How could they weep as they looked at that smile of perfect peace—that wonderful smile, fixed now in death, which had lightened up all her face as she cried out to Fritz with her parting breath, "Fritz, see!—it is all true—Violet has wings"?

Aunt Lizzie sat all day beside the little bed—yes, and all night too. She was never tired looking at the sweet pale face, so restful in its sleep; and though tears flowed constantly down her cheeks, her heart was ever busy thanking God, who had so mercifully called home his little suffering lamb before the last sad news had reached her of her father's death.

She was with them now, that was enough for her to know, and for evermore all would be peace. The little mother so long sighed for, the father who had so tenderly shielded his darling from trouble, and had watched over her in her loneliness—yes, they were all united now, and she knew that Violet was beyond the reach of trouble. For her and for them sorrow and sighing had fled away, and in their place had come the everlasting rest and happiness of heaven. No wonder that Aunt Lizzie rose up sometimes suddenly and kisséd the sweet face with a passionate thrill of joy, nay, almost of envy.

The neighbours streamed in all day long; indeed it seemed to Aunt Lizzie that the whole town of Edelsheim came to see the little face lying in such a sweet stillness on the pillow.

Beautiful white flowers were laid upon the counterpane, and the air of the room was almost oppressive with the scent of the violets which were brought as a last offering, as a last tribute of love to their own Violet, the sweet flower of Edelsheim, whose face had ever looked out upon them from the many-sided window overhanging the street, with the patient smile so familiar to their eyes.

In the evening, when all the rest were gone, Fritz stole in, leading Ella by the hand. Kate had just placed the lamp on the table, and Aunt Lizzie had risen up to draw the curtains; but he looked at neither of them, only walked over straight to the bedside, and stood there gazing at his little companion's face with an intense and speechless sorrow. But with Ella it was different. She gave one glance at the figure so unfamiliar in its stillness, and then fled with a cry to Aunt Lizzie, burying her face in her dress and sobbing violently.

Aunt Lizzie drew the little girl into the inner room to comfort her; Kate hobbled down the stairs sobbing as she went; and Fritz was left alone, still standing gazing with a bursting heart at the smile which was not for him.

For a moment he lifted his eyes and looked round the room nervously, and then he stooped and kissed her forehead. "Violet," he said softly, and waited, childlike, for an answer; but the lips did not move in response, only to his eyes, dazzled as they were with resisted tears, the smile seemed to widen at his call.

"Violet, hist! Fritz knows now that thou hast wings. Violet, Fritz loves thee; and, listen, Violet, Fritz will always, always remember thee; and he will always love God, too, and the good Lord Jesus." Two immense tears fell upon Violet's face; and then Fritz, drawing nearer, knelt down by the side of the little bed and covered his face reverently with his hands.

When Aunt Lizzie returned to the room Fritz was gone, but the tears which the boy had shed still glimmered faintly on the quiet face.

That evening, too, the old policeman came to take
his last look. He stood with uncovered head by the
bedside, and uttered not a word. The face seemed to
have a strange attraction for him, for he gazed at it
without moving for many minutes. He, too, kissed
his little friend ere he walked away, and laid in the
cold clasped hands a bunch of blue forget-me-nots.
But at the door he paused, and looking at Aunt
Lizzie he asked, with an eye which for the moment
burned with a suppressed anger, "Where is the
girl ? "

"Dost thou mean Evelina ? "

"Yes, certainly."

"Ah, she has returned to Gützberg ; she left here
the very evening of the accident. She feared, I
think, to meet the face of any one who knew and
loved our darling."

"Ah, she did well," he said bitterly. "God, who
forgives all sin, may pardon her. He can be merciful
as well as just. But we of Edelsheim, never ! "

The next morning the carriage, made with such care
by poor faithful John, was lifted out from its corner
in the room and carried down into the street ; and
there they laid upon it the little white coffin which
held the body of Violet.

The descent to the little church-yard near the fountain was densely packed with mourners, and with difficulty the old policeman, assisted by Fritz, drew it through the weeping crowd. Behind it walked a company of children dressed in the same white robes with the same white wings which they had worn on the day of the procession; and now, as the little carriage moved on, their lips opened, and there burst forth the same song of the angels welcoming the weary soul to heaven which had startled Violet from her reverie only a few short days before, and had called her from her loneliness and her fear to everlasting life.

Thus her wish was fulfilled, that her first drive in the carriage made for her by her father should be to the place where her mother had been buried; and there they laid down the poor tired lamb at last, to sleep on its mother's breast. The people, gathered round the grave, sobbed and wept; the angels lifted up their voices with the same sweet but mournful cry; the policeman folded his arms on his breast, grim and stern, while his sword clinked against the gravel. But it was left for Fritz to know the whole grand truth. Standing there unconscious of all and everything around him, with eyes uplifted to heaven he saw her as she was.

White-winged, rejoicing, exulting in her new-found
strength, poised in the air above his head, radiant in
robes of dazzling whiteness, he saw again that small
white face break into a smile of rapture; and he heard
a voice say, "Fritz, 'no more tears;'" Violet has
wings." And then some one cried out, "Look at the
boy! he is white as death, he is fainting;" and so
they lifted him into the church and laid him on the
ground, and Aunt Lizzie placed his head upon her
knee.

And by-and-by the crowd dispersed, and those who
lingered laid wreaths upon the grave; and some knelt
down and kissed the earth above their little Violet's
sleeping-place.

                *   *   *   *   *

It is now many a long year since little Violet
escaped out of her cage and mounted up like a bird
to heaven, and yet she is remembered as lovingly as
ever by the people of Edelsheim. If you turn aside
into the little church-yard at the foot of the hill, you
will see the monument that they have erected with
much love and care to her memory. And perhaps you
may meet there a woman who comes often to weep at
her grave and to pray, but from whom the towns-
people still turn away with aversion. She is never
tired looking at the white face carved so faithfully

and beautifully in marble, nor at the outstretched pinions which, spreading across the arms of the cross, support the cherub's head.

There is no epitaph to tell of their darling's pure life, nor of her sad death ; only three words, and yet they embrace all—" Violet has wings."

It was Fritz who chose them. But to comfort the hearts of all those in Edelsheim who had loved her so well, the sculptor added at the base of the monument a bunch of fading violets, and beneath them he carved these words of hope and consolation— " Auf wiedersehen " (To meet again).

THE END.

CPSIA information can be obtained at www.ICGtesting.com
Printed in the USA
BVOW021116270213

314319BV00015B/317/P

9 781167 047978